Easy Rider

Lee Hill

 Publishing

First published in 1996 by the
British Film Institute
21 Stephen Street, London W1T 1LN

Reprinted 2004

The British Film Institute promotes greater
understanding and appreciation of,
and access to, film and moving image
culture in the UK.

British Library Cataloguing-in-Publication Data
A catalogue record for this book is available
from the British Library

ISBN 0-85170-543-X

Series design by Andrew Barron
& Collis Clements Associates

Typeset in Italian Garamond
and Swiss 721BT by
D R Bungay Associates,
Burghfield, Berks

Printed in the USA

BFI Modern Classics

Edward Buscombe and Rob White
Series Editors

Advancing into its second century, the cinema is now a mature art form with an established list of classics. But contemporary cinema is so subject to every shift in fashion regarding aesthetics, morals and ideas that judgments on the true worth of recent films are liable to be risky and controversial; yet they are essential if we want to know where the cinema is going and what it can achieve.

As part of the British Film Institute's commitment to the promotion and evaluation of contemporary cinema, and in conjunction with the influential BFI Film Classics series, BFI Modern Classics is a series of books devoted to individual films of recent years. Distinguished film critics, scholars and novelists explore the production and reception of their chosen films in the context of an argument about the film's quality and importance. Insightful, considered, often impassioned, these elegant, well-illustrated books will set the agenda for debates about what matters in modern cinema.

Contents

In Memoriam

Alfred Hill (1933–1982)

Acknowledgments

This book grew out of research for a longer work-in-progress, but specific contributions to this project cannot go unnoticed. Since this is partly a book about giving credit where credit is due, I would like to highlight a number of generous and kind individuals. For their information, friendship, hospitality and support: John Baxter, the staff of the BFI Stills, Posters and Design Department, Victor Bockris, Phil Coombs, Gail Gerber, Stephen and Colin Gilmour, David Godwin, Jean Hartard and Leslie Needham, Patrick McGilligan, Joseph McGrath, Tom McSorley at the Canadian Film Institute, Michael O'Donoghue (1940–1994), Scot Morison of Alberta Foundation For The Arts, Perry Richardson, Nile and Carol Southern, Jean Stein and Damon Wise. For their enthusiasm, encouragement and patience, Ed Buscombe and Rob White of BFI Publishing. For sharing research and inviting me to participate in their documentary, *Born To Be Wild*, Nick Jones and Kelly Axton of the BBC. For their love and help beyond the call of duty, Esther and Claire Hill and Patty Johnson.

And finally, it is doubtful this book would have been written without the inspiration of the original grand guy, Terry Southern (1924–1995), whose wit and seriousness have kept my eyes on the right road.

1 Going to Mardi Gras: The Making of Easy Rider

... the idea was to pick a town, such as the one we were in, and then to sort of drive away from it, in the opposite direction, so to speak. I knew what they had in mind, more or less, but it did seem in being this strong on just-wanting-to-get-away-from, we might simply end up in the sea or desert. Then, too, at one point there was a kind of indecision as to the actual direction to take, left or right – so I suggested that we look at a map.

From Terry Southern's 1962 short story, 'Road Out of Axotle'.

Easy Rider was the little road movie that came out of nowhere to change Hollywood forever. Or so goes one of film culture's most enduring myths. Upon release, the film became an essential part of 60s iconography, embodying the hopes and fears of the time. As the first blockbuster hit of the Hollywood New Wave, *Easy Rider* influenced the direction and attitudes of future moguls, George Lucas and Steven Spielberg, as well as mavericks such as Terrence Malick, Francis Coppola and Martin Scorsese. Since 1980, the optimism and vigour of American film-making have fallen away as part of the wider decline of international cinema's idealism. *Easy Rider*'s success did indeed point audiences, critics and film-makers in a new direction, but the diminishing returns of 80s and 90s cinema indicate that the New Wave was largely a road not taken.

Nevertheless, *Easy Rider* has remained that rare beast: the commercially successful cult film. As a favourite of repertory screenings and revivals, as well as a popular home video rental, nostalgia alone can not explain *Easy Rider*'s subversive appeal as the ultimate road movie. Neither its humble budget, nor its bleak tone and ultra downbeat ending prevented it from earning over $60 million world-wide.[1]

Easy Rider's plot synopsis – two hippie bikers travel across America after a big cocaine sale – could be a high-concept pitch made by the likes of Don Simpson and Jerry Bruckheimer. But in the late 60s, drugs, sex, rock 'n roll and casual violence were subjects and themes that the major studios felt puzzled, if not downright threatened, by.

Easy Rider's impact was made possible by a bold synthesis of the disparate styles, moods and practice with which 60s pop culture was awash. The acting paid homage to the Actors Studio and the groundbreaking experiments of John Cassavettes' *Shadows* (1959) and Shirley Clarke's *The Cool World* (1963). The self-conscious use of the camera, especially the jump-cuts and zooms, also displayed the influence of the work of the various European new waves then flooding American art houses and film societies – the British Free Cinema, the French *nouvelle vague*, the Italian neo-realists from Antonioni to Fellini and the Czech New Wave. The editing built on the frenetic cutting of Richard Lester and mid-60s television advertising, and the cinéma vérité of D. A. Pennebaker and Richard Leacock. The underground films of Jonas Mekas, Stan Brakhage, Andy Warhol and others suggested seemingly infinite possibilities of cinematic expression, some of which *Easy Rider* exploited and developed. The film's use of songs by Jimi Hendrix, The Band and other groups reflected the growing importance of rock music as a sophisticated complement to film narrative. Dennis Hopper's and Peter Fonda's 'apprenticeship' on Roger Corman's B-Grade youth pics accounted for *Easy Rider*'s budget and scale.

Behind the making of *Easy Rider* was an uneasy, but passionate, collective driven by the flow of contradictory ideas and emotions that dominated the 60s. The disparate backgrounds of Fonda and Hopper, screenwriter and novelist Terry Southern, co-producers Bert Schneider and Bob Rafelson, Jack Nicholson, Lazslo Kovacs and Henry Jaglom, among others, led to varying degrees of conflict. Yet the communal ethos of the decade kept the creative disagreements and one-upmanship in check until the film was completed and released.

Like many films that become surprise hits, *Easy Rider* grew out of complicated and sometimes contradictory motives. The idealism of Hopper and Fonda was coupled with self-righteousness and paranoia. The urge to experiment and innovate was underpinned by a shrewd instinct about what did and did not work in the emerging youth market. *Easy Rider*'s success would become a symbol of what independent and personal film-making in America could be. Yet this was also a film made by men who had been raised and trained in the heart of mainstream Hollywood studio production, who had had access to the establishment against which they subsequently rebelled. The genesis and making of *Easy Rider* amply illustrate how revolutions are rarely simple or pure.

On 27 September 1967 Peter Fonda was in a Toronto hotel room resting from doing the rounds at Showrama, a convention of US and Canadian distributors. He was there to publicise *The Trip*, made that year by Roger

Peter Fonda
publicising
Roger Corman's
The Trip.

Corman for American International Pictures. Surrounded by publicity material, Fonda lit up a joint and stared at a photograph from another Corman film, *The Wild Angels* (1966), of him and Bruce Dern standing in front of motorcycles. Whether it was just the dope or idle rambling inspired by fatigue, Fonda suddenly had a revelation. He and Dern were modern cowboys! Instead of John Wayne or Gary Cooper, he saw two hip guys travelling across America on bikes experiencing the freedom of the road. As the image came into deep focus in his mind, he saw Hollywood's version of the grail – the idea for a hit movie.

Shortly after this epiphany, Fonda phoned his friend Dennis Hopper, another uneasy fringe player watching the Old Hollywood lumber on. He told Hopper, who was considering giving up the movie business to teach acting, about reworking the ideas from the Corman biker films to create a modern Western. Fonda knew Hopper harboured directorial ambitions. As well as acting in *The Trip*, Hopper had shot some promising second-unit footage in the desert. Fonda persuaded Hopper that this genre hybrid would be a perfect vehicle for their respective debuts as producer and director. They would also share the lead roles. Hopper, no stranger to wild and sudden enthusiasms, was hooked. When Fonda returned to Los Angeles, the two met for a series of manic planning sessions at Fonda's home.

Despite the mistrust that later dominated the production, Hopper and Fonda were an ideal pairing. They had been raised within Hollywood's studio system, but they also shared the myriad interests and concerns of 60s counter-culture. They felt their careers were stifled and inhibited by the expectations the studios still had of young actors with Middle American good looks. It sounds like a joke now, but by simply growing their hair long, they had seriously impaired their careers in the eyes of studio casting agents and producers. Their choices were narrowing to exploitation pictures or supporting roles as misfits and villains.

As the son of Henry Fonda, the quintessential Hollywood good guy from *Grapes of Wrath* (1940) to *Twelve Angry Men* (1957), and brother to Jane, the rising 60s sex symbol of *Cat Ballou* (1965) and *Barefoot in the Park* (1967), Peter had an onerous legacy of fame and success to cope with. Like his sister, he was still troubled by the suicide of his mother, Frances Seymour Brokaw, Henry Fonda's second wife. His relations with his superstar father were complicated by feelings of failure, inadequacy and neglect. As a boy, he attended a prestigious private school, but a fight with another student led to his expulsion. After this he was sent to Henry's home town in Omaha, Nebraska, where he was raised by his aunt and uncle. He studied acting at the University of Omaha and appeared in several student productions. In 1961 he won a lead role in the Broadway play *Blood, Sweat and Stanley Poole*. The play was not a hit, but his acting was singled out by the New York Drama Critics Circle which called him the year's most promising young actor. The acclaim, his good looks and famous last name led to a starring role in the innocuous *Tammy and the Doctor* (1963). His next two films, Carl Foreman's World War Two melodrama, *The Victors*, and Robert Rossen's *Lillith* (both 1964), opposite Warren Beatty and Jean Seberg, were more prestigious and challenging. Yet he hadn't created the excitement the industry or audience expected of someone with the Fonda name.

The American International films *The Wild Angels* and *The Trip* gave Peter the breathing room to find out what kind of Fonda he really wanted to be. Under the guidance of Roger Corman, an industrious and thrifty producer/writer/director, Fonda made two of the best American International films produced for the youth market. What these films lacked in budgets, publicity and studio prestige, they made up for in energy, economy of style and freshness of talent. *The Wild Angels* was a nihilistic portrait of a motorcycle gang that could almost have been a documentary recreation of Hunter S. Thompson's book *Hell's Angels*. *The Trip* was also first-rate Corman. It pretended to document the evils of drug experimentation, but was largely a mystical character study heavily influenced by Fellini and Bergman. As a director of commercials, Fonda is given LSD under the supervision of a sympathetic friend played by Bruce Dern and undergoes an identity crisis. Scripted by Jack Nicholson, another gifted Corman protégé, the film threatens to fall apart after each everything-but-the-kitchen-sink hallucination. However, a scene in which Fonda runs down Sunset Boulevard in a drug frenzy is startlingly conceived. The neon signs, storefront advertising, billboards, music pouring out of discos, and motor traffic all conspire to drive Fonda mad. The film's inspired montage was an early instance of the combination of photography, music and editing that would make *Easy Rider* so potent.

Like Fonda, Hopper found the Corman films a refuge from career problems and a workshop to learn and develop a new style of film-making. Hopper was born on 17 May 1936 in Dodge City, Kansas, a small town immortalised in countless Westerns. After his father's return from the army at the end of World War Two, the family moved to San Diego. Hopper began acting in the city's Old Globe Theatre and won attention during his teens for his Shakespearean roles. At the age of eighteen, he was given a traditional studio contract at Columbia, but he resented the attempts of Barry Cohen, the head of production, to groom him. He ended up at Warner Bros., where he acted in *Rebel without a Cause* (1955) and *Giant* (1956), opposite James Dean. Dean became a role model for Hopper. He encouraged Hopper to pursue outside creative interests such as painting, photography and literature. Dean's death in a car crash on 30 September 1955 accelerated Hopper's more destructive impulses towards rebellion and self-expression. After refusing to play a scene a certain way for Henry Hathaway in *From Hell to Texas* (1958), the director retaliated by shooting countless takes until the young actor caved in and then had him blacklisted by the studios. Although Hopper was married to Brooke Hayward, daughter of the agent Leland Hayward and actress Margaret Sullivan, the blacklist limited him to television work in Los Angeles and New York.

True to Dean's outlaw spirit, Hopper flourished. From the late 50s through the mid-60s, he made enough money to collect art, hang out with various bohemian friends such as Allen Ginsberg and Robert Frank and participate in radical causes and events. He organised an opening for Andy Warhol. He played a love-struck sailor in Curtis Harrington's underground film *Night Tide* (1961). He marched to Montgomery, Alabama, with Martin Luther King. His photographs of various emerging musicians, writers and painters appeared in such magazines as *Vogue* and *Harper's Bazaar* (collected in the book *Out of the Sixties*, published in 1986), while his marriage to Brooke Hayward was intriguing enough to inspire Harrington's feature *Games* (1967), starring James Caan and Katherine Ross as a similarly hip couple. It was an interesting period, but Hopper missed the intensity and focus of making movies on a regular basis.

Hopper and Fonda were both frustrated by their film work to date. As they talked out their story, variously dubbed *The Loners* and

Dennis Hopper appeared in *Giant* with his mentor, James Dean.

Mardi Gras, they grew hopeful that it would break up the stasis of their careers. They discussed the logistics of raising a modest budget. Although Hopper was recently divorced from Brooke Hayward, her brother, Bill, came on board as Fonda's partner in the newly formed Pando Productions and to assist with financing. Fonda flew to the south of France to meet his sister, Jane, and brother-in-law, director Roger Vadim, and co-star in the 'Metzengertsetin' episode of the anthology film *Spirits of the Dead* (1967). But Jane and Vadim were still completing *Barbarella*, the erotic science fiction spoof, at Cinecitta studios in Rome so work on *Spirits of the Dead* could not begin immediately. During this interlude, Fonda met Terry Southern, who was rewriting much of *Barbarella* for Vadim. Southern would become essential to the development of *Easy Rider*.

By 1967 Terry Southern had become a legendary 60s personality, the hipster's hipster. Born on 1 May 1924, in Alvarado, Texas, Southern served with the US Army in Europe during World War Two. After the war, he completed a BA in English literature at Northwestern University in Chicago. Then he went to Paris on the GI Bill to study at the Sorbonne. Instead of completing a thesis, he dedicated himself to becoming a writer. He wrote short stories for expatriate magazines such as *Zero* and *The Paris Review* and was encouraged by William Faulkner, Nelson Algren and Henry Green. By the end of the 50s, the novels *Flash and Filigree* and *The Magic Christian* had established his cult reputation as a gifted and original satirist. In 1964 the mainstream success of the meta-porn novel *Candy* (co-written with Mason Hoffenberg) and his work on *Dr. Strangelove* (1963) with Stanley Kubrick and Peter Sellers had made him a hero of the counter-culture on a par with Jean-Luc Godard, the Beatles, Bob Dylan and William Burroughs. In person, Southern vacillated between courtly shyness and wild outrageous humour. His expansive wit and generosity won him friends in the mainstream as well as the underground. Southern knew everyone from the Rolling Stones and Lenny Bruce to Kenneth Tynan and George Plimpton.

Southern already knew Hopper and Fonda as part of a charmed circle of kindred spirits that by the mid-60s floated buoyantly between Los Angeles, New York, London, Paris and Rome. Southern and Hopper shared mutual friends such as London gallery owner Robert Fraser and Jean Stein (the daughter of MCA founder Jules Stein). Southern would often see the Fondas and Vadim at the weekend gatherings they hosted in Malibu, where the still unknown Jack Nicholson would drop by with Robert Walker Jr. At one time, Jane was on Southern and Frank Perry's shortlist of candidates to star in the film of *Candy* before the project fell under the humourless direction of Christian Marquand.

Southern was also one of the hottest screenwriters of the period. He had worked with Tony Richardson on *The Loved One* and Norman

Terry Southern
(with Ringo Starr)
on the set of
The Magic Christian,
adapted from
his novel.

Jewison on *The Cincinatti Kid* (both 1965), as a script doctor on
Casino Royale and *Don't Make Waves* (both 1967), and was considering
producing his own films, including an adaptation of *A Clockwork
Orange*. He was one of a kind, a hip man of letters who loved the
possibilities of film.

Fonda told him about the project he was trying to launch.
According to Fonda, Southern was immediately enthusiastic: 'That's a
great story. I'm your man.' Fonda was taken aback by the prospect of
hiring Southern as his screenwriter. His mid-60s fee was around
$100,000 per script. Generous to a fault, however, Southern agreed to
work for scale (roughly $350 per week) and also lend Hopper and
Fonda's independent production the legitimacy of a name screenwriter.[2]

By late November, Fonda, Hopper and Southern were meeting at
Southern's 55th Street office in New York for regular story conferences.
According to Southern, Hopper and Fonda's idea for a movie was still
embryonic:

**Very early on it was called *Mardi Gras* to identify it. The first notion
was that it be these barnstorming cars, stunt driver cars, where
they do flips and things, but that just seemed too unnecessarily
complicated. So we just settled for the straight score of dope, selling
it and leaving the rat race. We forgot about the daredevil drivers
which is a commonplace thing. It was going to be this troupe who
play a few dates and places and eventually get fed up with that and
make this score. Finally, we forewent any pretense of them doing
anything else than buying cocaine. We didn't specify that it was
cocaine, but that's what it would be. They go to New Orleans to sell
it. Then once they got their money, they ride to coastal Florida or
some place like Key West where they could buy a boat cheap,
not in New Orleans, because it would be too expensive.[3]**

Fonda and Hopper were writers only in the sense that they could talk up
a storm. Southern would ask them questions, make suggestions and also

tape their conversations. A secretary made typed transcripts of their meetings. (The secretary was also a devotee of UFOs and entertained the trio with her fervent belief in flying saucers and secret bases in Mexico.)

Southern worked this found material and notes from the story conferences into a vivid shooting script with highly specific camera directions and rich naturalistic dialogue. Fonda and Hopper would play two stunt riders, Billy and Wyatt a.k.a. Captain America, who buy cocaine in Mexico and sell it for a profit to a big dealer in Los Angeles. With their money hidden in Wyatt's gas tank, they would travel through the south-western United States to their 'place in the sun' in Key West. On this picaresque journey, they come into contact with ranchers, townspeople, various authority figures and members of the counter-culture, who react with varying degrees of sympathy or hostility. After being jailed on a minor charge in a small Texas town, they are bailed out by an eccentric civil rights lawyer, George Hanson. He joins them on their trip so he can visit a legendary New Orleans brothel, Madame Tinkertoy's. Tragically, the gentle and open Hanson is killed when the trio's campsite is ambushed by a group of locals. Arriving in New Orleans, they find Mardi Gras in full tilt. At Madame Tinkertoy's, they hire two prostitutes and convince them to take in the festival. The four drop an LSD tab that was given to Wyatt at a commune and embark on a series of hallucinations akin to a near-death experience. In the final scene of the script, Wyatt and Billy are back on the road travelling faster than ever towards their dream in Key West. Two men in a pick-up drive by the two bikers. They intend to scare the two 'long hairs', but their shotgun blast accidentally hits Billy and he crashes. As Wyatt rides back to assist his fallen comrade, the pick-up circles back. Wyatt is also gunned down. The gasoline tank on his bike explodes. Both script and film end with:

LONG SHOT from above as the old pick-up truck turns around again and drives down the desolate highway leaving in the ditch the two

bodies and the wounded chrome bike which, as distance lengthens, continues to burn with a small bright glow.[4]

Southern's extensive work and input were played down by Hopper and Fonda after *Easy Rider*'s release in favour of the more exotic notion that the screenplay was largely improvised. Neither Hopper nor Fonda, however, disputed that Southern came up with the title, a gritty colloquialism for a man who lives off the earnings of a whore.[5] The title was a stroke of genius: simple, imagistic and allusive. It reinforced the basic pitch of two bikers 'on the road' but also focused the idea that America had become lazy and materialistic in its pursuit of money at all costs.

'The idea of meeting a kind of a straight guy, which turned out to be the Jack Nicholson role, was totally up to me,' Southern recalled.

I thought of this Faulkner character, Gavin Stevens, who was the lawyer in this small town. He had been a Rhodes scholar at Oxford and Heidelberg, and had come back to this little town to do whatever he could there. So I sort of automatically gave the George Hanson character a similar sympathetic aura. I wrote the part for Rip Torn, who I thought would be ideal for it. When shooting began, we went to New Orleans and Rip was going to come, but he couldn't get out of this stage commitment.[6]

Hopper's concept of Hanson was inspired by a drinking buddy, Jack Sterritt, a graduate of the University of Texas who later directed Fonda in *Race with the Devil* (1975). Torn was the favoured choice for the Hanson role (although Bruce Dern was also considered). Torn and Southern had been friends since meeting on the set of *The Cincinnati Kid*. A versatile actor and, like Southern, a Texan, Torn understood Hanson's milieu and the ambivalence such a sensitive and intelligent man would feel living in a parochial world prone to racism and intolerance. One of the many myths that have surrounded the making of

Easy Rider is that Torn walked off the set of the film and had to be replaced by Jack Nicholson at the last minute. This is simply not true. The reality was far more mundane. While Torn did in fact read the script, he had a commitment to act in a play by Jack Gelber which overlapped with the designated shooting dates. He was also wary of Hopper's mercurial personality and role as first-time director. Nevertheless, one version or another of 'the walk out' would persist in press coverage for years to come and seriously affect Torn's career in the 70s. After *The New York Times Magazine* regurgitated the story on 12 October 1977, Torn forced the newspaper to print a full retraction: 'Mr. Torn has informed the magazine that while he was asked to read the script of *Easy Rider*, he never agreed to play any role in the film and was never on the film set, and, therefore, never "walked off the picture".'

As the script was being completed, *Easy Rider* moved from being a potential American International film to a pick-up for Columbia Pictures. Corman's partner, Samuel Z. Arkoff, wasn't crazy about the druggy anti-heroes and wanted Hopper either to act or direct, not both. Jack Nicholson, who seemed to socialise with everyone in the emerging New Hollywood, suggested they take the film to Raybert, a production company run by Bob Rafelson and Bert Schneider.

Rafelson and Schneider became the godfathers of *Easy Rider*. Schneider's father, Abe, was a Columbia executive, and his brother, Harold, was head of production. Schneider worked in the television section of Screen Gems, a Columbia subsidiary, for several years until, quitting his job, he moved to Los Angeles, where he became partners with Rafelson. Rafelson, a philosophy graduate from Dartmouth College and Benares University in India, had worked as a television writer and story editor. Their company, Raybert Productions, created the group and accompanying TV series, *The Monkees* (1965–7). This packaging coup made all concerned very wealthy. When Rafelson and Schneider heard the pitch for *Easy Rider*, they were producing a Monkees film, *Head* (1968), an odd quasi-Brechtian parody of their cash cow, co-written by Jack Nicholson and directed by Rafelson. Rafelson and Schneider became the brokers between Columbia and Pando Productions. They were able to give Fonda and Hopper the go-ahead on the film as long as they stuck to the modest budget of $365,000. In return, they would receive a third of the film's profits, with Columbia and Pando splitting the remainder.

At this stage, no one envisioned the film doing anything more than breaking even. Columbia had almost no experience of reaching the youth market. In 1967/68, their major releases included *Guess Who's Coming to Dinner, The Night of the Generals, Divorce American Style, To Sir, with Love, Hammerhead* and *Funny Girl*. Some of these films were hits, but others either barely covered the studio's overhead or were outright flops. The directors and producers behind these films tended to be middle-aged play-it-safe craftsman. Their films tried to mirror topical concerns, but the stilted results were at best detached, or at worst hopelessly modish as was the case with *The Happening* or Jerry Lewis's swinging London film, *Don't Raise the Bridge, Lower the River.*

Before a production team could be assembled for principal photography, and before the completion of the shooting script, a crucial portion of the film had to be shot for logistical reasons: Fonda had mixed up the dates of the Mardi Gras festivities in New Orleans and thought there was a month to spare. So, on 23 Feburary 1968, Hopper and Fonda went to New Orleans with an *ad hoc* 16mm camera crew including documentarian Les Blank and Seymour Cassel, a member of Cassavetes' repertory, to shoot what became the Mardi Gras acid trip sequence. Toni Basil and Karen Black were cast to play the two prostitutes Billy and Wyatt pick up at Madame Tinkertoy's.

Perhaps overwhelmed by lack of preparation for his first day in the directing chair, Hopper struck many in the small team as dictatorial. 'On the first day,' Fonda recalled, 'he gathered us in a parking lot and shouted "This is my fucking movie!" at the top of his voice repeatedly.'

Fonda and the others were so fed up that they shot some of the film without him that first day.[7] That evening, Terry Southern arrived from his home in Connecticut and sat in on a tense meeting. As Hopper argued with the cast and crew, Southern listened with weary patience. At one point, he drawled, 'The cacophony of your verbiage is driving me insane.'[8]

An estimated sixteen hours of footage was shot over the next five days on the streets of New Orleans and in a local cemetery. Much of it was ad-libbed, although Southern supplied some striking suggestions for the acid sequence in a rewrite:

Ghost figures of parades in off colors through multiple optical illusions. Dark areas of umbrellas. In tearing the clinging objects of clothing from her body, MARY finds new freedom in the light that bursts from wrought-iron crosses ... They [one of the men and MARY] wallow in the mire and in open tombs.[9]

Everybody seemed to be pointing a camera and shooting film regardless of their experience. In some cases, rainwater got on the film as cartridges were being changed. Yet these accidents resulted in dappled and refracted images. This unintentional effect heightened the sense of an acid trip being recreated.

In another example of inspired chaos, Hopper goaded Fonda to talk about the effect of his mother's suicide as if he were stoned. It was the kind of personal experience that most actors would recoil at having to deal with. Fonda relented as Hopper wore him down with various aesthetic arguments. It was crude and callous, but the results made the completed sequence as authentic as it was harrowing and surreal.

After the near disaster of the New Orleans shoot, there was a lull to reorganise the production. Southern withdrew most of his input to work on two other projects, an adaptation of his novel *The Magic Christian*, and *End of the Road*, a film he was going to co-produce in New England with Aram Avakian. From this point onward, the creative and logistical battle over the film would be waged between Fonda and Bert Schneider on one side, and Hopper, in the manner of von Stroheim, on the other. 'There was only one creator there,' Hopper has since said, 'I was a dictator, I wouldn't listen to anybody. It was a case of get out of my way, this is how we're going to do it.'[10] Clifford Vaughns, an associate of Fonda's, wrote to Southern about the production's volatile climate: 'I am still quite concerned about your involvement in the film. It seems to me that you not only have much to contribute creatively, but also in terms of providing a stabilising influence in the direction of the production.'[11]

By the end of February, the shooting script was ready. Hopper and Fonda hired Paul Lewis as their production manager and assistant director. Lewis had cut his teeth on some of the Corman productions and worked with Jack Nicholson on the low-budget existential Westerns *The Shooting* and *Ride the Whirlwind* (both 1966), directed by Monte Hellman. After scouting locations across the southern States with Hopper, Lewis began to organise a camera crew, with Laszlo Kovacs as director of photography.

Laszlo Kovacs, along with Vilmos Zigmond, who would become another great cinematographer of the 70s, was trained at Hungary's Academy of Theatre and Film Arts. Kovacs and Zigmond graduated from the four-year course in June 1956. In October the Hungarian Revolution broke out and was suppressed. The two fled to the USA and sold 16mm footage of the revolution to CBS Television for $10,000. They then spent years in the wilderness of odd jobs before getting their respective breaks. Kovacs was lucky enough to be hired on a nudie picture, which led to work on educational films. Richard Rush hired Kovacs to photograph a low-budget exploitation film, *A Man Called Dagger* (1967). Kovacs worked on *Psych-Out* and *The Savage Seven* that same year and was pretty well burnt out by their limitations when Lewis called. Lewis reassured him that *Easy Rider* would be different.

Kovacs recalled Hopper's return from New York, script in hand, for the first production meeting: 'Hopper said, "Don't worry about the script. I don't want anybody to read the script. Everybody sit down and I'll tell you the story."' Hopper's manic spiel captivated Kovacs and the others at the meeting, but he was also impressed with the written material: 'We had a very specifically written script by Terry Southern, Dennis Hopper and Peter Fonda. All the scenes were carefully followed, especially the dialogue sequences after the Jack Nicholson character joins them. It wasn't just a bunch of stoned guys sitting around a campfire improvising that.'[12]

The next five weeks of principal photography were fraught with tension. Fonda and Hopper seemed to be in constant conflict. They both shared the same vision of the movie, but fought over who had final authority on the set. This tension, compounded by the enormous amount of cross-country travelling, made for long, gruelling days of shooting. Yet the filming was completed on budget thanks principally to the professionalism of Kovacs and Lewis and a crew assembled from the relatively cheap NABET television union.

Kovacs supervised the whorehouse interiors on a Columbia soundstage. Then the sequences involving the back story – the stunt riding, making the score in Mexico, being chased by police, meeting the Connection played by Phil Spector, hanging out at a drive-in movie theatre, a brawl with other bikers – were shot on location in Los Angeles or on backlots. (Many of these scenes would be discarded in the final cut.) The commune sequence was filmed in Topanga Canyon.

Schneider persuaded Hopper and Fonda to cast Nicholson in the George Hanson role. Nicholson was well aware he was at the right place at the right time. Although he knew Hopper, Fonda, Rafelson and Schneider, as well as Southern, by being on the fringe of the Los Angeles–Malibu scene, his distinct acting persona had taken almost a decade to evolve. Hard work and determination had taken the former lifeguard from Neptune, New Jersey, to Los Angeles in the late 50s, where he worked as an office boy in the MGM cartoon department. He studied in acting classes run by Jeff Corey and was given small roles in various low budget films (more often bad than good). By the age of thirty-two, his future as an aspiring actor was less than encouraging. His only big-budget role, as a flower child in Vincente Minnelli's *On a Clear Day, You Can See Forever* symbolised everything he hated about mainstream Hollywood. His screenwriting efforts were both more promising and more true to his values. He was extremely proud of his scripts for *Head*, *Ride the Whirlwind*, *The Shooting* and *The Trip*.

Hopper was reluctant to use Nicholson. He couldn't picture him as a Texan, but Nicholson cut his hair and dressed for the part. When he arrived at the location in Texas, he knew his lines verbatim. Nicholson understood George Hanson was the heart and soul of the film and as such a golden opportunity for any actor. His assurance and commitment shone through in all his scenes. He was also, much to everyone's relief, funny and easygoing.

Dennis Hopper overseeing Laszlo Kovacs' photography.

Throughout the remainder of the shoot during March and April, roaming through California, Arizona, Texas, New Mexico and Louisiana, Fonda and Hopper tinkered with parts of the script. Fonda wanted to make his character more enigmatic and reduced his dialogue to clipped sentences. Hopper thought his role was to ask questions and therefore drive the story forward. Southern, still the film's literary mentor, was told of these changes and was less than pleased. In a letter of 24 April, he complained to Fonda about the 'dumb-bell dialogue'. Fonda's rewrites on the whorehouse scene struck Southern as useless:

I am certain that you will remember that probably the worst scene in The Trip was the 'merry-go-round' scene where Dennis ran off at the mouth, trying to explain things to the audience, instead of to the person he was talking to ... whereas one of the *very best* scenes in the movie was the one in which he was talking *exclusively* to the other character, i.e., the scene in which you come back to his pad, and he questioned you saying: 'Man, I can't tell if you're still high or if you're putting me on.'[13]

In this Southern anticipated the chief criticism of the film's detractors. Fonda and Hopper often mistook silence and inarticulacy for naturalism. But, as shooting ended and editing began, Southern was by now only one of many auteurs on *Easy Rider*.

Hopper assembled a four-hour rough cut. Henry Jaglom, an aspiring actor and creative type friendly with Schneider and company, was hired to consult on the editing on the basis of an 8mm film he made of the Six Day War in Israel. Jaglom was bored by the endless travelling shots of Fonda and Hopper on their bikes. Schneider and Fonda agreed, but liked their balletic quality. They also wanted to heighten the film as a visual, non-verbal experience. Everyone agreed that Kovacs' cinematography was a triumph. He had shot the American road with a poetry, sensitivity and insight reminiscent of photographer Robert Frank's *The Americans*.

Donn Cambern was the official editor on the film, and along with Jaglom, Schneider, Rafelson, Fonda and Nicholson tried to bring the film down to the 90-minute to two-hour length suitable for commercial release. Hopper was persuaded to take a holiday at his home in Taos, New Mexico, while various cuts were tried out. At one point, according to Jaglom, he was in a room editing the film from the end, and Nicholson was in another room editing from the beginning. Nicholson didn't want to edit scenes he appeared in, so Jaglom worked on them.[14]

In addition to the aforementioned cuts, the road trip out of Los Angeles edited to the full length of 'Born to Be Wild' (with billboards providing ironic commentary) was dropped. Ten additional minutes of the volatile café scene in Louisiana and extended versions of all the campfire scenes were cut. The brothel scene, which as scripted by

Jack Nicholson, who cut his hair for the part of George Hanson, preparing for filming.

Southern was longer, was also pruned. Hopper was aghast when he saw the new assembly. 'You've ruined my movie,' he told them. The others managed to persuade him that they were maximising the potential of all his hard work. Some of Hopper's notions (which he would take to the limit two years later in *The Last Movie*) were unworkable. Southern recalled, for instance, that Hopper wanted the opening screened upside down, but was persuaded that this Brechtian device would alienate not just the straights who ran the studio, but also the hip, young audience to whom the film was addressed.[15]

On the other hand, Hopper convinced his collaborators to drop a commissioned score by Crosby, Stills and Nash and use the songs he laid down for his cut. Hopper's choices proved to be an essential part of the film's success. The music of Steppenwolf, The Byrds, The Band, Holy Modal Rounders, Jimi Hendrix, The Electric Flag and others is a vivid snapshot of the fusion of styles that typified American rock in the late 60s and was clearly chosen by someone who was a part of the counter-culture.

One artist didn't want Hopper and Fonda to use his song. Bob Dylan was shown a cut which used his classic song 'It's Alright Ma (I'm Only Bleeding)' over the final credits. Dylan hated seeing the biker anti-heroes get killed by the rednecks. He suggested Fonda's character survive and drive his bike into their pick-up. Dylan was missing the point, Hopper and Fonda argued: this wasn't a film about revenge. Eloquent arguments for and against inclusion of the song went on until Dylan relented. They could use his song, but not over the credits and only if it was sung by Roger McGuinn. He then offered them some new lyrics which he spontaneously scrawled on a piece of paper. 'Give this to McGuinn, he'll know what to do with it.' McGuinn added a verse and completed 'The Ballad of Easy Rider', an original that became the film's elegaic coda.[16]

Hopper was also allowed to sculpt the New Orleans acid trip footage with Cambern. According to Cambern, this was the last scene edited for the film. 'It was tremendously wild footage,' Cambern recalled, 'While editing the film, there was a part of me always working on that acid scene.'[17] Cambern and Hopper chose abrupt, straight cuts to heighten the hyper-reality of a trip, as opposed to the then more conventional use of dissolves, solarisation and optical effects. It was the section of the film best served by Hopper's visionary impulses.

———

Throughout 1968 Hopper and Fonda screened the film for friends and associates. Mike Nichols and Michelangelo Antonioni were both early champions of the film. *Easy Rider* was invited to the Cannes Film Festival as the official American selection. Southern was originally going to be the sole screenwriter credited with the film's story, but during this stage he was approached by Hopper and Fonda with a request he share writing credit. Against the advice of the Writers Guild of America, who had won the right strictly to limit directors angling for such credit, Southern agreed to their request believing, at the time, that a three-way credit accurately reflected the collaborative spirit behind the venture. He also felt it would make it easier for them to produce future projects. It was an act of goodwill Southern would regret.[18]

Easy Rider's premiere at Cannes on 13 May 1969 was met with a stunned silence and then a standing ovation. Although the Palme d'Or went to Lindsay Anderson's *If . . .*, a poetic allegory of late 60s rebellion, Hopper was named the best new director. The *Variety* reviewer Gerald Maskowitz described the film as 'perceptive' and predicted it would 'appeal to both youthful and selective audiences, with art chances promising. Peter Fonda name an asset, plus firm directorial debut of Dennis Hopper.'

Easy Rider's first American screening was on 10 July at the Museum of Modern Art. The film opened in America on 14 July. Vincent Canby in the *New York Times* was one of the less enthusiastic critical voices. While he admired the production values, Canby wrote in his review of 15 July, 'It's pretty, but lower case cinema.' He felt the film never quite recovered from Nicholson's departure early in the film's third act. This was a minority view. As the film went into major release, it proved to be a runaway hit and the fourth highest-grossing picture of 1969, raking in more than $19 million that year. By contrast, number five, 20th Century-Fox's big-budget musical *Hello Dolly* had cost $26,400,000 and grossed only $15,200,000. Columbia executives, who were previously embarrassed by *Easy Rider,* were now scrambling to imitate it as a model for box-office success.[19]

Easy Rider received two Academy Awards nominations: for best supporting actor (Jack Nicholson), and best original screenplay. Many critics instantly hailed the film as the start of a new American cinema. Some of the hyperbole obscured the vitality of film throughout the subsequent decade. Prior to its release, there had been many films which

'*Easy Rider* was showing not only where Heaven and Hell might be located but, more agonisingly, where the Fall had begun.'

captured the 60s dramatic surges of hope and despair. Stanley Kubrick, John Frankenheimer, Mike Nichols, Sidney Lumet and Arthur Penn were not much older than Hopper and Fonda and broke many of Hollywood's rules with such films as *Dr. Strangelove* (1964), *The Manchurian Candidate* (1963), *The Graduate* (1967), *The Pawnbroker* (1964) and *Bonnie and Clyde* (1967). Nor were all studio veterans bereft of innovation. Alfred Hitchcock's *Psycho* (1960) was arguably more revolutionary than *Easy Rider* in the way it created a new grammar for genre film-making.

The awareness of foreign film was at its zenith at the end of the 60s thanks to the impact of Bergman, Fellini and Truffaut on middle-class audiences. Yet for many in the autumn and winter of 1969/70, *Easy Rider* was more than just an exciting new film to see. This was a road movie that drove right through many people's hearts. It was a confirmation that post-war history was at a watershed. The 60s had witnessed unparalleled social, economic and cultural change. If there was a motto for the decade, it was 'nothing is true and everything is permitted', a slogan which sums up the counter-culture's dream of a secular paradise. Faithful to this dream, but with a resigned pessimism, *Easy Rider* was showing not only where Heaven and Hell might be located but, more agonisingly, where the Fall had begun.

2 The Ballad of Easy Rider

A question in your nerves is lit / Yet you know there is no answer fit to satisfy / Insure you not to quit / To keep it in your mind and not fergit / That it is not he or she or them or it / That you belong to
Peter Fonda's favourite lines from 'It's Alright Ma (I'm Only Bleeding)' by Bob Dylan.

A man went looking for America, but couldn't find it anywhere
Ad copy from *Easy Rider* poster.

Together with his collaborators, Peter Fonda turned *Easy Rider* into something more than a modernised Western. *Easy Rider* is an 'Eastern' which reverses, questions and rejects the expansionist impulses many Americans held sacred prior to the 60s. As Wyatt and Billy drive in-country away from Los Angeles, California, the end of the frontier, becomes, to use William Burroughs' great phrase, the end of the human line. The idyll of 'the big score' proves as transitory and misleading as the golden dreams that derail the characters of the novels of Theodore Dreiser and F. Scott Fitzgerald. In spite of occasional lapses into obscurity, *Easy Rider* sustains its tragic vision of roads that eventually turn in on themselves or come to early and abrupt termination.

From beginning to bitter end, this simple story of two bikers on the road resonated with viewers in 1969 in a number of ways. The plot of the film may appear almost schematic at times, but its politics are far from simple. As *Easy Rider* was being written and filmed during 1967 and 1968, the mood of the 60s was undergoing an irrevocable shift. While only those with a bad sense of history would recall the decade as a simple time of sweetness and light, there was a strong consensus that those outside the status quo could fight for positive change and progress. During *Easy Rider*'s production, the idealism of the 60s had so far weathered the assassination of John F. Kennedy, the escalation of military involvement in Vietnam and racial strife in major American cities. Harold Wilson's Labour government in the UK still enjoyed the glow from its 'white heat' of revolution. Lyndon Johnson's Great Society had not yet been derailed by partisan bickering in the Democratic Party. And the series of strikes and protests that rocked France in May 1968 underscored the belief that power truly was falling into the hands of the people.

But this belief proved to be founded on false optimism. In 1967, the year of the Summer of Love, from love-ins in San Francisco and Amsterdam to the Beatles singing 'All You Need Is Love', there was also the Six Day War between Israel and Egypt, civil war in Nigeria and the increasing deployment of US troops in Vietnam. Anti-war demonstrations were increasing in number and the tone of protest growing more militant. 1968 exploded in violence with the Tet Offensive, the assassinations of Robert F. Kennedy and Martin Luther King, rioting in American ghettos and university campuses, the street fighting and protests that shattered the Chicago Democratic Convention, and the Soviet invasion of Czechoslovakia. The feeling of collapse intensified through 1969 as the Vietnam War continued, and the counter-culture began to fall apart in the aftermath of the Manson murders and the disastrous Rolling Stones concert at Altamont speedway.

The makers of *Easy Rider* seemed to have known instinctively that the notion of the 60s as a decade of idealism, progress and hope for the future was as fragile and delicate as a strip of celluloid. Billy and Wyatt discover that the decade's optimism is akin to a brief, promising mirage like oil shimmering on the road's horizon. The reactionary fear of the Silent Majority, championed and goaded by Richard Nixon and Spiro Agnew in the 1968 presidential campaign, emerged as the more dominant response towards the social and cultural change of the 60s. The hostile political climate was not helped by the fact that the militant politics of the Black Panthers, the Weathermen and the more pugnacious members of Students for a Democratic Society tended to inspire confrontation rather than understanding or co-operation.

In capturing this turmoil, *Easy Rider* reverses the premise of most Westerns. Traditionally, the lawlessness of the frontier is shown being tamed by the individual, family or state. It was John Ford's genius in *The Searchers* (1956) and *The Man Who Shot Liberty Valance* (1962) to show that such civilising forces had their price, but even his revisionism asssumed that the frontier's taming was inevitable and necessary. The Native Americans who preceded the calvary, settlers and various commercial interests were the first to be made to submit to this new order and the last to share in its benefits. Their resistance was seen as the response of savages. Although in more liberal Westerns, they are depicted accepting the compromise of government reservations, or assimilation as guides, farmers or 'good injuns', even these films do not question the principles of expansionism and industrialisation.

Easy Rider's narrative, however, begins with a rejection of technocracy, an abandonment of the cities built since the West was won. Partially influenced by Herman Hesse's *Journey to the East*, one of many novels by the German writer reissued in the 60s, Fonda wanted Billy and Wyatt's odyssey from Los Angeles to Key West to illustrate the rootlessness, loss of spirituality and destruction of nature created by America in the 20th century. As their journey unfolds, Billy and Wyatt would come to realise the materialism of their motives and yearn for deeper values and goals.[20]

Billy and Wyatt are named after two quintessential Western characters, Billy the Kid and Wyatt Earp. Wyatt, with his long and enigmatic silences, is clearly the more thoughtful of the two. Unlike Billy, Wyatt doesn't instantly fear or distrust the people they meet on their journey. He compliments the rancher (Warren Finnerty) who invites them to dinner on his good fortune at having a healthy family and a self-sustaining piece of land. He accepts the donation of gas from the hitchhiker (Luke Askew) without suspicion. At the commune, Wyatt admires the determination of its inhabitants. Watching them trying to till the barren soil, he utters the startlingly naive line, 'They're going to make it.'

Nevertheless, Wyatt won't or can't commit himself to any of these possibilities for growth and change. His reflective passivity borders on narcissism. His sympathetic words and actions can't quite disguise his calculation and lack of direction. Although we don't know who originated the decision to buy the cocaine in Mexico, Wyatt is probably the one with sufficient intelligence and calmness to have developed the plan.

If Wyatt is a rebel in search of a cause, Billy is clearly one without a clue. Like the rednecks and townies who harass them, he is unworldly and paranoid. One of Hopper's greatest contributions to the film is to play Billy with humour and subtlety. A less intuitive performer might have emphasised Billy's greed and antagonism, but Hopper shows him as a simple young man terrified of losing his shot at the good life. Billy is attracted to the promise of sex, drugs and rock n' roll, but the touchy-feely slogans and confusing relationships of the commune offer him little, if any, pay-off. In this, he is probably like the majority of those who grew up in the 60s who enjoyed the party, but who were ultimately concerned with personal survival rather than social change.

Wyatt and Billy are amoral drifters united by the money hidden in the gasoline tank and their final destination in Florida. Their redemption comes through their association with George Hanson. As the film's moral centre, Hanson transforms the self-interest and solipsism of Wyatt and Billy. He represents the 60s ideal of a figure who can bring together liberal and conservative, reactionary and radical, for the sake of friendship, community and the common good. Naturally, he must come to a terrible end.

As revealed in the brief, but compact dialogue in the Texas jailhouse, Hanson comes from a wealthy family, but his politics – he has worked for the American Civil Liberties Union – extend beyond his privileged upbringing and the town's parochialism. He has a drinking problem and worries what his parents will think of his rowdy behaviour. To the sheriffs, he is a combination of village idiot, fellow good-old-boy and civic leader. To Wyatt and Billy, he is initially just their ticket to freedom. But then he becomes something greater, the holy fool who will save them from themselves.

Jack Nicholson's performance is astonishing. Hanson is empathetic, insightful, witty, passionate, spontaneous, aware of his faults and open to new ideas. Although Terry Southern was thinking of Faulkner's tragic heroes when he fleshed out the Hanson character, one wonders if Nicholson's interpretation was a discreet homage to the screenwriter who shared many of Hanson's charming traits. Hanson is only in a quarter of the film, but his presence is so warm and charismatic that even critics who hated *Easy Rider* were won over by the character and Nicholson's performance.

Hanson's dialogue in the jailhouse and around the campfire explicitly articulates the film's political subtext. His first exchange with

The confrontation between the counter-culture and the rule of law.

Billy and Wyatt reflects the conflict between idealism and cynicism and the drive to reconcile these opposing forces. After Billy apologises for reacting violently to being woken by Hanson in the jail, George replies, 'Oh, that's all right. There's no misunderstanding – we're all in the same cage here.'[21] Unlike Wyatt, who flirts with 60s idealism at the commune, Hanson is an activist. He is using his law degree and wits to keep the Silent Majority and counter-culture from coming to blows. The dialogue suggests he has probably spent much of the 60s keeping civil rights workers from being lynched, hippies from being tarred and feathered, and the constitutional rights of his fellow citizens from being trampled by authoritarian zeal.

In his famous 'this used to be a helluva good country' speech, Hanson shows that he understands the decade better than Wyatt and Billy, who wear all the trappings of the counter-culture. Billy thinks the intolerance he has encountered is motivated by his long hair and dress, but Hanson knows the fear goes deeper. The images of non-conformity and experimentation now dominating the 60s threaten the conventional limits of freedom in a materialistic society. Hanson defines the fear of these changes with chilling clarity:

... talking about [freedom] and being [free] – that's two different things. I mean, it's real hard to be free when you are bought and sold in the marketplace. 'Course don't ever tell anybody that they're not free, cause then they're gonna get real busy killin' and maimin' to prove to you that they are. Oh yeah – they're gonna talk to you, and talk to you, and talk to you about individual freedom, but they see a free individual, it's gonna scare 'em.

It is interesting to note that the sentiments expressed in this speech are echoed in 'Red Dirt Marijuana', a subtle and penetrating short story written by Southern and published in *The Evergreen Review* in 1960. Set in rural Texas in the 30s, it deals with the friendship between CK, a black ranch-hand, and Harold, his white boss's twelve-year-old son.

(Overleaf) Billy and Wyatt turn their backs on American technocracy.

CK turns Harold on to the simple pleasures of home-grown marijuana, but tells him why smoking the weed is outlawed:

Well, maybe you're too young to know what I talkin' 'bout – but I tell you they's a lotta trickin' an' lyin' go on in the world ... they's a lotta ole *bull-crap* go on in the world ... well, a man see right through all them tricks n' lies, an' all that ole bull-crap. He see right through there into the *truth* of it![22]

In a related story, 'Razor Fight', CK is killed in a barroom brawl with another black man. To Harold's father, he is just another second-class negro destroyed by drinking and gambling. To Harold, CK's death reveals white society's tacit acceptance of various forms of benign slavery and oppression. Consciously or subconsciously, Southern used the Hanson character in *Easy Rider* to amplify his rage and disgust at the self-serving hypocrisy many Americans had made, and continue to make, of freedom, equality and the pursuit of happiness.[23]

Arguably the smartest creative decision Hopper and Fonda made was to bring in Southern to sustain this undercurrent of dissent. He provided a foundation which made the improvisations that occurred during filming logical extensions of the script and not just lucky accidents. What becomes clear through the comparison of script and film is how Southern in his detailed characterisation of George Hanson had a more profound understanding than either Hopper or Fonda of what the real themes of *Easy Rider* were.

The ninety-page shooting script carefully wove in Wyatt and Billy's back story through dialogue. Originally the film opened with Wyatt and Billy performing motorcycle stunts at a country fair. They are almost ripped off by a sleazy promoter who tries to pocket the bulk of their takings. As written this opening was no more than four to five minutes in length, but it added poignancy to Wyatt and Billy's desire to 'make the big score'. This sequence was shot on a backlot in Los Angeles, but discarded. When they sell the cocaine to the big-time dealer (Phil

Spector) at the end of the runway at Los Angeles International Airport, expository dialogue was dropped in favour of the ominous roar of jet engines. As stated earlier, a longer prologue showing Wyatt and Billy evading a helicopter border patrol in Mexico, setting up the sale, waiting and hanging out in a drive-in, on the beach and in a Sunset Boulevard coffee shop were also edited out during post-production.

These cuts arguably improved the overall pace of the film, but the motives for the cocaine sale and the resulting journey have to be taken on faith and imposed by the viewer. Less sympathetic viewers might be inclined to see Billy and Wyatt as nothing more than dangerous long-haired creeps who sell drugs. Such open-endedness is what makes many films so rich and rewarding. However, it should be said that while Jean Renoir may have argued that everyone has their reasons, his films

Connection (Phil Spector) buys cocaine from Billy and Wyatt.

made a strong effort to supply specific clues as to *what* those reasons might be, and this is not always the case in *Easy Rider*'s final cut.

In the script, Southern also helped Hopper, Fonda and Kovacs develop the visual strategy for the film. Not all of his ideas were used, but many were shot. For example, the credit sequence that shows Wyatt and Billy driving out of Los Angeles originally intercut billboards and streets signs with travelling shots of them on their bikes. This montage was intended to underscore the rampant hucksterism found in the landscape of the modern American city. Southern's shooting script also indicates how the opening and other travelling shots should be paced:

TECHNICAL NOTE: In this scene we establish (1) Wyatt's 'colors' (2) the chromed container where the money is concealed in Wyatt's gas tank (3) the sleeping rolls (4) the pack and preparation for the journey – all done in a series of QUICK CUTS with MUSIC and NO TALKING.[24]

As in the final cut, the script shows Wyatt throwing away his watch – a literal and symbolic rejection of the constraints of time and space associated with urban life. However, before they visit the farmer with his Mexican wife and scores of children, there were two intriguing encounters which weren't used. In the first, Wyatt and Billy exchange pleasantries and briefly ride with a group of black bikers. The only black Americans seen in the final cut are glimpsed in travelling shots, living in roadside shacks (another deleted scene would have shown a black farmer letting Wyatt, Billy, and George camp on his land after the taunts in the roadside cafe). In the second, while refuelling at a gas station, Billy and Wyatt become the objects of vocal scorn by a typical suburban mom and dad with 2.5 kids.

It is conjecture whether the inclusion of these scripted scenes would have made a better film. The editing is generally so accomplished that even without these intriguing episodes, we get a vivid sense of how America's natural beauty, democratic traditions and regional diversity stand side by side with poverty, inequality, racism and provincialism. For the most part, the shooting script and final cut differ only in detail and together reinforce the complex of characters, themes and imagery that made *Easy Rider* the template for road movies to come.

––––––––––

The roads and highways Billy and Wyatt speed across bring them into contact with a startling diversity of characters symbolising the contradictions of the deeply sought, yet highly elusive American Dream. The nature of these encounters is almost always transitory as the promise of the Dream keeps moving farther down the road. As the prototype for so many road movies to come, *Easy Rider* establishes a narrative tradition that will often be defined by characters adrift in a confusing landscape of nostalgia, broken promises and regrets, abandonment and interruption, and destinies too elliptical to recognise or too terrible to bear.

In the countless road movies that have followed *Easy Rider*, the protagonists rarely arrive at their destination or find what they are seeking. The diversions and sidetracks become ends in themselves and the original inspiration for hitting the road is lost or irreparably fragmented. Whereas the classical odyssey ended in a homecoming, the attainment of a hard-won goal or a reconciliation of sorts, the post-*Easy Rider* road movie deals with characters who are orphaned in some fashion, and confronted by the elusiveness or futility of their dreams and various manifestations of alienation. A kind of hip anomie-under-pressure envelops the characters of far too many road movies, blunting the genre's mythic underpinnings. Yet in the hands of a thoughtful and passionate director, the road movie can be more than a genre-bending romp through the fields of pop nihilism. Wim Wenders' *Paris, Texas* (1984) and Jim Jarmusch's *Down by Law* (1986) are two such examples, with characters who transcend rootlessness and rediscover their link to the rest of humanity.

Given *Easy Rider*'s bleak and fatalistic ending, it is intriguing that many viewers and critics recall the film as an artifact of 60s idealism rather than as a harbinger of the increasingly cynical tone of the decades to come. Perhaps this is because the stops and rests that Billy and Wyatt make on the road offer a counterpoint to the grim trajectory of the storyline. In subsequent road movies, from Monte Hellman's *Two Lane Blacktop* (1971) to Ridley Scott's *Thelma and Louise* (1991), these diversions are increasingly defined as brief respites from an inevitable acceptance of what cannot be changed. Even in Albert Brooks' witty parody, *Lost in America* (1985), the road trip of two unemployed yuppies, which is directly inspired by their youthful memories of *Easy Rider*, fails as an alternative to big-money jobs and conspicuous consumption. What makes *Easy Rider* so pivotal in the emergence of this very modern genre is how the film juxtaposes its anti-heroes' attraction to idealism and commitment with their tendency towards self-interest and hedonism. On the one hand, *Easy Rider* celebrates the liberating grandeur of an epic journey into the unknown. On the other, it criticises the vanity and selfishness of individuals who pursue narcissistic goals over the values of friendship and community.

Before George Hanson is killed, one watches *Easy Rider* with the hope that Billy and Wyatt will exchange their place in the sun for something more meaningful discovered along the way. As they ride through the myriad highways and backroads of the American Southwest, they are given the opportunity to embrace a number of different social organisations and moral systems.

Ironically, given their outlaw status, one of the first of these opportunities comes in the person of the laconic but friendly rancher who invites Wyatt and Billy to join his family for dinner. The rancher is an idealised figure (he is not intimidated in the slightest by the odd appearance of his guests), who clearly practices the conservative values he believes in. He embodies freedom and responsibility unsullied by prejudice, hypocrisy or pretense. Wyatt is clearly attracted to the rancher's simple life of hard work, family and traditional Catholic beliefs and compliments the rancher: 'It's not every man who can live off the land. You're doing your own thing in your own time.'

The scene suggests the possibility that the two bikers could become hired hands or even use the drug money to buy farmland themselves. But it also hints at a gulf between the rancher and the bikers. The rancher has stayed in one place to build a life for himself and his family. Billy and Wyatt are restless and impatient, almost extensions of the bikes they ride, and only truly selfless when speeding down the road towards a seemingly endless horizon.

By contrast, the commune exists on the opposite end of the spectrum from the world of the rancher. The commune, an old idea recast by 60s utopianism, is far from perfect. Its mood is balanced precariously between the coy self-consciousness of the actors from the

Billy and Wyatt embrace none of the alternative possibilities of living offered to them.

Gorilla Theatre and the uncritical submergence in various Eastern philosophies practised by the Robert Walker Jr. character who blesses the communal meal. The less than insightful Billy is perceptive enough to realise that the knowing smiles hinting at an undertow of mind and power games wouldn't be easy to deal with either (he's generally made uneasy by the commune). The sexual politics are dubious – the women seem to do all the cooking. The crop being sown looks doomed. There is no ignoring the commune's flaws, but the experiment is brave, sincere and life-affirming. The commune is significant to our understanding of Billy and Wyatt because it is such a specific and defined example of 60s counter-culture. Billy and Wyatt dress and talk like the inhabitants of the commune and are accepted without fear and prejudice. Yet Billy remains distrustful, while Wyatt is curiously non-committal in spite of his appreciation and sympathy for their experiment in living.

In the original shooting script, it is made clear that Wyatt falls in love with Lisa, one of the women Billy and he meet and go skinny-dipping with. He considers staying. The commune and the possibility of a relationship with Lisa suggest more challenging and problematic commitments than those on offer at the ranch. But in both cases what is at stake is a direct engagement with the world which Billy and Wyatt reject. For Billy, the commune is just a pit-stop to get free food and drugs and maybe some recreational sex. When Billy balks at giving the two women a lift, Wyatt reprimands him: 'You're eating their food, man.' Yet Wyatt's admiration for the commune doesn't really extend beyond a few perfunctory compliments. Like Billy, Wyatt is compelled by the money in the gas tank to continue their journey deeper into the South.

When they are thrown into jail after crashing the parade, the next possibility of hope is represented by George Hanson who, like them, stands apart from the mainstream but is not part of the counter-culture. Unlike them, he is a participant in his times, albeit a somewhat angry and world-weary one. Even if Wyatt and Billy could never contemplate living in a small Texas town, they are, in principle at least, capable of learning from George's ability to transcend his parochial surroundings through charity, humour, tolerance and generosity.

After helping to win Wyatt and Billy's release, George decides to join them so he can visit Madame Tinkertoy's, a legendary New Orleans brothel, recommended by the governor of Louisiana himself. George may look like a straight arrow, but he sympathises with the counter-culture that rural America finds threatening. But, like Wyatt and Billy, George is only human. In the roadside cafe, where they are faced with the crude epithets of the locals, including a sheriff, even Hanson's grace and courage are defeated by the insults, veiled threats and intimidation. Anyone who watches the film more than once can't help wishing Wyatt, Billy and George would keep on riding after they flee the cafe or, better yet, catch a plane to somewhere safe like Greenwich Village or Swinging London. Anywhere seems safer than below the Mason–Dixie Line in 1968.

The unlikely trio doesn't get too far and Hanson pays the ultimate price for his brief friendship with Billy and Wyatt. His death at the hands of locals – people whom George probably shares more in common with than Billy and Wyatt – is a tragic confirmation of the despair that informs *Easy Rider*'s reading of the 60s. Viewers in the late 60s could all too easily make parallels between Hanson's death and the assassinations of Robert Kennedy and Martin Luther King, and the deaths of the young and innocent in Vietnam, and connect this to the increasing disillusionment of the Silent Majority with Lyndon Johnson's Great Society and the willingness to embrace the law-and-order ethos of Richard Nixon.

As *Easy Rider* progresses, Billy and Wyatt's journey down the road becomes not just a flight from the pressures of the city and the restrictions of mainstream society, but an escape from prickly questions of conscience and responsibility. Billy and Wyatt evaluate and define what they see strictly as individuals in transit. What sustains the momentum of their journey – all that money coiled like a snake in Wyatt's gas tank – is rarely discussed. The drug money which seemed to promise liberation instead heightens their restlessness and diminishes their capacity to define their goals except in broad strokes. Billy and

Wyatt are only at ease during the campfire scenes which offer rare
opportunities for reflection and discussion, as well as disturbing portents
of things to come.

In the first campfire scene, the mood is so relaxed and low key as
to seem inconsequential, but it does set up the opposition between Billy
and Wyatt. Billy sings about 'going down to Mardi Gras to get me a
Mardi Gras queen' and getting more food, dope and sex to keep him
happy. Wyatt is quiet and simply says, 'I'm just getting my thing
together.' Billy is clearly the more materialistic of the two, while Wyatt
seems to be wondering if there is more to the big score than simply
instant gratification.

The next campfire scene, set in Pueblo ruins, involves the stranger
from the commune. Billy is suspicious of where he is leading them.
'Where are you from, man,' he repeatedly prods the stranger. The
stranger is evasive and finally just replies, 'the city'. He then reprimands
Billy for not being more respectful of the Indian graves lying beneath
them. Wyatt barely reacts in this scene, but there is a clear sense he
trusts the odd serenity and conviction of the stranger.

The two campfire scenes with George are, it barely needs to be
repeated, the most endearing and heart wrenching. Hanson's 'the
Venusians are among us' rap is a hilarious respite from the distrust and
earnestness which colour many of Billy and Wyatt's exchanges. The
three men laugh, talk and get stoned together without reservation or
resentment. The brief time the two bikers spend with George represents
the closest they come to attaining the sense of community that is missing
in so much of the country they travel through.

The next campfire scene follows the ominous stop at a roadside
cafe. The three are verbally harassed by redneck locals and leave without
being able to order even a cup of coffee. Around the campfire that
night, George, in reference to the ugly mood at the roadside cafe,
becomes sad and regretful as he discusses the cruel reality of American
freedom. After they go to sleep they are ambushed by some of the same
locals from the cafe and beaten with baseball bats. Billy manages to

Companionship is undercut by sadness in the campfire scenes.

scare the intruders off, but he and Wyatt are injured and George is killed. They bury George and decide to visit Madame Tinkertoy's as a kind of homage to their travelling companion.

The death of George Hanson turns their road trip into a race towards oblivion. Reaching New Orleans, they eat at a fancy restaurant and go to Madame Tinkertoy's. Billy is in seventh heaven now that they are finally spending some of their money on good times, but Wyatt is weary and remote. He convinces Billy and the two prostitutes, Mary and Karen, to join him on a tour of Mardi Gras festivities. Encouraged by the kaleidoscope of drunken high spirits, costumed revellers, music, parades and partying that makes up Mardi Gras, this quartet forms a tight but temporary bond. The two women are probably the same age as Billy and Wyatt and not dissimilar in terms of class or background. All four are blue-collar fringe players on the counter-culture. They stagger together towards the cemetery and embark on an acid trip. The LSD, which was given to Wyatt by the stranger at the commune, becomes a sacrament of disillusion and self-negation. But as the acid trip sequence intensifies, the drug provides little peace or enlightenment. The revelations which the drug induces appear to be made of excruciatingly painful memories associated with each character's unique sense of failure, loss and solitude.

The final campfire scene is filled with a mood of desolation. The shallow purpose of their journey, remorse over Hanson's death, and the dissatisfying bacchanal of Mardi Gras have taken their toll on Wyatt, while Billy remains oblivious to the spiritual costs the two have paid in their pursuit of the big score:

BILLY: We've done it. We're rich Wyatt. Yeah, man, yeah. We did it. We're retired in Florida now, mister.
WYATT: You know Billy, we blew it.
BILLY: That's what it's all about man, you go for the big money and you're free. You dig?
WYATT: We blew it.

In the morning, the road unfolds for Wyatt and Billy one last time. The travelling shots show the Louisiana delta being polluted by the uncontrolled growth of American industry and consumerism. Factories, sprawling towns and freeways obscure the verdant landscape. Ironically, it is on one of the last stretches of relatively uncluttered road that the two bikers are killed.

What can be said about the death of Wyatt and Billy that measures up to watching those final seconds of gunfire and explosions? Unlike the bloody slow-motion denouements in *Bonnie and Clyde* and *The Wild Bunch,* two very different and powerful ruminations on American violence, the ending of *Easy Rider* is sudden, catastrophic and banal. The camera floats up from Wyatt's burning bike, evoking images of the carpet bombing by American planes in Vietnam seen on television news programmes and documentaries. The credits begin to roll. A long, wide river can be seen alongside the highway, extending into a horizon of clouds and haze and finally disappearing.

Over the credits, the simple refrain of Roger McGuinn's 'The Ballad of Easy Rider' – 'the river flows, it flows to the sea, wherever it flows, that's where I want to be' – is heard. McGuinn sings of a man who only wanted to be free. The song aligns freedom with the beauty and grandeur of America's natural landscape. Yet the grim deaths of Billy and Wyatt make it impossible for viewers to define freedom so easily. In America, at the end of the 60s, freedom had become a call to arms, an epithet, a lie and even a threat. Freedom had become everything except a salvation.

From the casual opening at the Bar Contenta in Mexico to the quick, indiscriminate killing at its conclusion, *Easy Rider* maintains an almost seamless documentary air. In their feature debuts as director and producer, Dennis Hopper and Peter Fonda succeeded in creating a powerful visual experience. The cinematography, rapid and concise editing, and minimalist dialogue may have been encouraged by the impact and success of Stanley Kubrick's *2001: A Space Odyssey*, which was in general release during 1968. The primacy of the visual opened

(Overleaf) 'The idealism of the 60s, like the money in Wyatt's gas tank, was too easily acquired and taken for granted.'

Easy Rider up to accusations of shallowness, pretension and obscurity. But, as was the case with *2001*, the ensuing controversy encouraged multiple viewings.

Compared to Kubrick's austere and meditative vision of the future, *Easy Rider* can be crude, occasionally incoherent, smug and self-indulgent. The short and clipped dialogue is something of an error in strategy. The shooting script and rough cut were more verbose. America is a nation of talkers, but the richness of regional voices is muffled in the film. The townspeople are almost always stereotypical rednecks, who only need the slightest provocation to form a lynching party (originally in the script's full-length cafe scene, an argument broke out between the men and the teenage girls who are sympathetic to the bikers). The women in the film, although realistically played by Luana Anders, Karen Black and Toni Basil, are only supporting characters. Their presence at the commune is only sketched in, while Mary and Karen, the two prostitutes, are never heard from again after the acid trip. And, of course, there are no speaking parts for blacks in the film. George Hanson refers to the racism of the South, but he is, after all, a privileged white liberal. The absence of a significant dialogue scene or encounter with a single black man or woman was a missed opportunity to expand the film's critique of the American Dream.

Certain ambitious visual ideas don't always pay off. The juxtaposition of the rancher shoeing his horse with Wyatt and Billy fixing a flat on their bikes is too literal. Hopper's use of flash-forwards to heighten the transition of time and space is erratic. Sometimes it works to great effect, especially in Madame Tinkertoy's when we get a glimpse of the biker's fiery death, but in many cases a simple cut would have done. The travelling shots are wonderfully hypnotic, but they often go on too long. More scenes of Wyatt and Billy talking or meeting with people on the road would have been just as visually moving as long shots of sunsets and sky lines.

As the previous section of this book indicates, the origins of the film were not pure. A major studio was involved, not all of the crew was composed of young turks, while Fonda and Hopper had more connections to the old Hollywood than they would probably care to admit. However, over twenty years later *Easy Rider* remains a landmark in low-budget independent film-making. Of all the criticisms levelled at *Easy Rider*, the glibbest and least supportable is that it has dated. The film works not simply as a vivid snapshot of the late 60s, but as a prophecy of the cynicism and exhaustion of the decades to come. The episodic narrative manages to encompass an eclectic range of the decade's cultural ferment. The communes, the interest in Eastern religions, the heightened awareness of civil rights, the biker and hippie subcultures, sexual liberation, the widespread experimentation with drugs, the romance of hitchhiking, the ever-shifting colours and styles of fashion, and the relevance and immediacy of rock music are all economically woven into an ostensibly artless storyline. The same narrative is strong enough to show how many of these ideas and movements would eventually fail or run aground in the 70s, and become consumed by their polar opposites in the 80s and 90s. *Easy Rider* is a film about the contradictions of the American pioneering spirit and the sheer waste and destruction that lies behind so much of the ambition underpinning the American Dream. *Easy Rider's* visual splendour does not obscure its tragic argument: the idealism of the 60s, like the money in Wyatt's gas tank, was too easily acquired and taken for granted, until it was squandered and violently destroyed.

3 End of the Road

The director is in vogue today, due to a complex set of social and economic circumstances. The premise of this book is that the phenomenon will not soon peak and pass. Rather, I suggest that we are on the threshold of a technological and aesthetic revolution in movies which will inevitably restructure human consciousness and understanding. Accessibility of the means of production and changes in distribution and exhibition will democratize movies so there will be thousands made every year instead of hundreds. And the independent filmmaker, whether he's working in Super 8 or 70-mm Panavision, will be the nexus of the change to come.

Joseph Gelmis in the preface to his book, *The Film Director as Superstar* (1970).

If audiences and critics saw *Easy Rider* as a reflection of the deep fissures in American society, the Hollywood industry was simply trying to capitalise on the box-office potential of this new genre, 'the youth film'. Unlike the recording industry, the big studios had been very slow to reflect the concerns and tastes of the emerging post-war baby-boom generation. While films immediately preceding *Easy Rider* included *Bonnie and Clyde* and *The Graduate,* there were also *Guess Who's Coming to Dinner*, *The Dirty Dozen* and the Julie Andrews' flop, *Star!*. For all the subtle and imaginative genre reworkings of *Point Blank* and *Rosemary's Baby*, the studios favoured the big budgets of *Funny Girl*, *Paint Your Wagon* and *Dr. Doolittle*. It is fascinating how many of the studios persisted in making costly musicals when rock music had rightly or wrongly eclipsed Broadway. Even a pre-*Godfather* Francis Coppola was persuaded to make *Finian's Rainbow*.

During 1969–70, the only established Hollywood presence to significantly recognise the youth market was the innovative New York-based United Artists. Their handling of Arthur Penn's *Alice's Restaurant* and John Schlesinger's *Midnight Cowboy* (the first and only X-rated

picture to win a best picture Oscar) was astute, shrewd and, by
Hollywood standards, progressive. MGM had Michelangelo Antonioni's
Zabriskie Point, but the film's ambivalence towards the protest
movement and its action painting aesthetics made it a difficult sell even
among the under-thirty crowd. Apart from *Easy Rider,* the great date
picture of 1969 was George Roy Hill's *Butch Cassidy and the Sundance
Kid*. The Paul Newman and Robert Redford blockbuster was the
number one box-office hit of the year and cleverly supplied restless
audiences with a little bit of everything the 60s was offering: the
irreverence of Richard Lester, the elegant pop of Burt Bacharach, the
quasi-*nouvelle vague* of Claude Lelouch, and echoes of the violence to be
found more explicitly in the films of Arthur Penn and Sam Peckinpah.

In their insightful 1964 *Esquire* article, 'The New Sentimentality',

The American dream?

Robert Benton and David Newman (the authors of the screenplay for *Bonnie and Clyde*) cannily predicted the emerging youth market. Hardcore members of the counter-culture were a vocal minority, whereas the vast majority of the youth market was traditional, politically middle of the road, middle class, and only engaged in a mild flirtation with the decade's much touted radicalism. Nevertheless, even if the political and social awareness of this market would prove superficial and transient, it was an audience that remained open to suggestion for almost all of the 70s.

By the end of 1970, the full impact of *Easy Rider* and the New Hollywood was evident in a whole range of releases: *Catch-22, The Boys in the Band, The Strawberry Statement, M*A*S*H, Woodstock, Medium Cool, Ice, Husbands, The Great White Hope, Performance, Little Big Man, Tell Them Willy Boy Is Here, The Landlord, Getting Straight* and *The Revolutionary*. Leading the pack of this ground swell were the films made by BBS, a new company formed by Bert Schneider, Bob Rafelson and their new partner, Steve Blauner. *Easy Rider* convinced Columbia that Schneider and Rafelson were the marketing geniuses of the youth market. The studio signed BBS to an unusually liberal multi-picture production deal. The only stipulation was that any picture made by BBS should have a budget of not more than $1 million. This stipulation aside, Columbia had no input in the films beyond distribution.

This combination of creative freedom and modest budgets endorsed the kind of personal film-making *Easy Rider* symbolised. The autonomy at BBS exceeded even Orson Welles' extraordinary contract with RKO in the late 30s. Welles was a mentor of the BBS crowd. He was a friend of Jaglom, Hopper and the film journalist turned director Peter Bogdanovich. Welles' work-in-progress, *The Other Side of the Wind*, a film about the collision of Old and New Hollywood, contained a pastiche of the youth film as well as appearances by his BBS friends.

Although BBS's output was small, their films would encounter none of the resistance or tampering *Citizen Kane* (1941) or *The Magnificent Ambersons* (1942) faced. Rafelson's *Five Easy Pieces* (1970), co-written with Adrien Joyce (a.k.a. Carol Eastman), and Bogdonavich's *The Last Picture Show* (1971), adapted from a novel by Larry McMurty, were commercial and critical successes. *Drive, He Said* (1970) and *A Safe Place* (1971) featured the respective directorial debuts of Jack Nicholson and Jaglom. Both films were flops, but admired for their uncompromising form and content. The last BBS film, *The King of Marvin Gardens* (1972), directed by Rafelson from a script by *Esquire* film critic Jacob Brackman was a dark tale of two brothers set in Atlantic City in the dead of winter. It was not a success, but the acting of Nicholson, Bruce Dern and Ellen Burstyn won acclaim.

In 1973 Columbia's relationship with BBS management cooled after Abe Schneider, Bert's father, was replaced at the studio by David Begleman (who was later implicated in an embezzlement scandal in

Nicholson's success in the 70s included starring in Bob Rafelson's *Five Easy Pieces*.

1978). The company was quietly dissolved. The reclusive Bert Schneider, by now a very rich man thanks to his share of *Easy Rider*'s profits, decided to aid various political causes including the opposition to the Vietnam War, George McGovern's campaign to win the presidency from Richard Nixon, and the Black Panthers. He co-produced Peter Davis's documentary, *Hearts and Minds* (1975), a powerful study of the devastating effect the Vietnam War had on its young veterans, which won an Academy Award. His involvement in the industry would eventually slow down, but subsequent productions such as Nicholson's *Going South* (1978), Terrence Malick's *Days of Heaven* (1978) and the baroque Chinatown sequel, *Two Jakes* (1990), were never less than intriguing.

Fonda's and Hopper's respective projects after *Easy Rider* became famous for their very public failure. Fonda's *The Hired Hand* (1971) was a revisionist Western similar to Robert Altman's contemporaneous but more assured *McCabe and Mrs. Miller*. More mood than story, Fonda's film was lovingly photographed by Vilmos Zigmond, but did nothing at the box office. Hopper's *The Last Movie*, also released in 1971, resulted in the actor's second famous period of exile from the Hollywood mainstream.

Financed by Universal, and shot on location in the mountains of Peru, *The Last Movie* was almost just that for Hopper the director. Universal had greenlighted the film on the basis of *Easy Rider*'s success and a promising script by Stewart Stern, the screenwriter behind *Rebel without a Cause* (1955). Once in Peru, Hopper discarded Stern's work in favour of almost total improvisation. As he told one of many reporters who visited the chaotic set, 'I want to make the audience; I want to build a reality for them. Then, toward the end, I start breaking down that reality. So [*The Last Movie*] deals with reality.'[25] The 'reality' of the plot, such as it was, concerned a stunt man, played by Hopper, who remains on a remote location for a Western after filming is completed and blindly pursues a local prostitute.

As a crazed and angry end of 60s film-within-a-film, *The Last*

Movie is a fascinating bonfire of the vanities. Its most inspired images are of Peruvian Indians fashioning camera equipment out of wood and miming the motions of the departed film crew. However, the film is dominated by pale imitations of Brecht, Pirandello and Godard. 'Scene missing' cards, credits and alternative takes interrupt rambling improvisations promising emotional truths that never quite surface. In contrast to the intuitive assurance of *Easy Rider*, Hopper's grasp of the Hollywood myths and genres he intended to deconstruct in *The Last Movie* seems tenuous. Rejecting anything resembling narrative drive, Hopper's direction suffers from a lack of purpose worthy of the film's protagonist.

At the Venice Film Festival, *The Last Movie* had its defenders and won the Golden Lion. Universal hated the film and barely screened it

Hopper during the making of *The Last Movie*.

outside New York. Hopper's drug and alcohol abuse, combined with *The Last Movie*'s dismal commercial prospects, negated his achievements on *Easy Rider* in the eyes of the studios. Through the 70s and early 80s, Hopper lived in Taos and acted mainly outside the United States. He became the actor directors called when they wanted to epitomise some variant of gonzo extremism. This typecasting did result in a fascinating tableau of character roles in Jaglom's *Tracks* (1975), Wim Wenders' *The American Friend* (1977), and Francis Coppola's *Apocalypse Now* (1979) and *Rumblefish* (1983).

In 1980 Hopper was given another chance to direct. *Out of the Blue*, a runaway Canadian production, was in such bad shape that even a pariah like Hopper was preferable to the original director. The film is a gritty story of an alcoholic ex-convict's crude attempts to rebuild his dysfunctional family. His wife is a heroin addict and his teenage daughter is a delinquent punk rocker with an Elvis fixation. Unlike *The Last Movie*, it had a beginning, middle and end, but despite its built-in cult appeal, it, too, flopped.

By the mid-80s, the years of substance abuse conquered Hopper's iron constitution. Amazingly, after a difficult and lonely period of hospitalisation and recovery, he emerged in 1986 with three highly praised comeback performances: the psychotic Frank Booth in David Lynch's *Blue Velvet*, an alcoholic ex-basketball star in David Anspaugh's *Hoosiers,* and a deranged, aging biker in Tim Hunter's *River's Edge*.

The new and sober Hopper was given the go-ahead to direct *Colors* (1988), a proficient, almost anonymous tale of black and Hispanic street gangs in Los Angeles. Subsequent directorial efforts, *The Hot Spot* (1990), *Backtrack* (1991) and *Chasers* (1995), have been moderately successful, but lack the power or ambition of *Easy Rider*, or even, for all its faults, *The Last Movie*. Hopper's eclectic interests, workaholic ethos and energy do not rule out the potential of another classic, but it is his prolific acting appearances that now have the most impact, in small independents such as Mick Jackson's *Chattahoochee*

(1989) and John Dahl's *Red Rock West* (1993) as well as blockbusters such as *Speed* (1994) and *Waterworld* (1995). His politics have also altered during the often tortuous course of his career. The former advocate of radical politics is now a proud Republican and supporter of Newt Gingrich.

After lensing *The Last Movie* for Hopper, Laszlo Kovacs became and remains a highly sought after cinematographer. He has worked with a who's who of American directors including Steven Spielberg, Hal Ashby and Brian DePalma. Karen Black's acting career flourished in the 70s, most notably in *Five Easy Pieces* and *Nashville*. Henry Jaglom, perhaps the shrewdest artist and businessman of the *Easy Rider* team, used his family's success in Los Angeles real estate to secure a production and distribution company, Rainbow Pictures. His quirky low-budget films, from *Always* (1985) to *Venice/Venice* (1992), have made money even when their autobiographical themes have perplexed and alienated viewers and critics.

Terry Southern's next two screen credits were on *End of the Road* and *The Magic Christian* (both 1970). *End of the Road* is a neglected adaptation of the John Barth novel that further explored the political and social fallout of 1968. *The Magic Christian* lacked the cohesion of the source novel but acquired a similar cult status. Between 1970 and his death in 1995, Southern worked on over forty other projects, but only *The Telephone* (1987), directed by Rip Torn, was filmed. In 1976 he wrote an evocative adaptation of William Burroughs' *Junky,* with Hopper slated to direct, but the financing collapsed. After *Easy Rider*, this became an all too familiar and frustrating pattern in Southern's career in the 70s.

In 1982 Fonda raised money to develop an *Easy Rider* sequel called *Biker Heaven.* Set in a post-apocalyptic future, Wyatt and Billy would come down from heaven to recapture the flag. Southern collaborated with Michael O'Donoghue and Nelson Lyon on a screenplay that was to be a dark and satiric extension of the first film. But as O'Donoghue pointed out, the options for a sequel were limited:

**The killer was you are dealing with just too many nutty people
involved who all wanted their own particular vision, and you are dealt
this card where the characters in the original are two dead hippies.
Then what happens? Heh, heh. 'Two dead hippies dead from a shot
gun blast lying on the road in the South. Then what happens, Mike?'
'Well, I don't know. Maggots begin to infest their shallow grave? The
nitrogen cycle?' You *really* have to take it in some bizarre direction.[26]**

Not surprisingly the studios passed on *Biker Heaven*. By the mid-80s,
Hollywood was dominated by play-it-safe big-budget blockbusters with
happy endings. Southern continued to get assignments and teach, but
his mix of angry satire and gentle irony was too rich a taste for the
studios and their perception of the market.

Clearly it was Jack Nicholson who benefited the most from the
success of *Easy Rider*. His acting dominated the 70s. In addition to his
BBS work, his performances in *Carnal Knowledge* (1971), *The Last
Detail* (1973), *Chinatown* (1974), *The Passenger* and *One Flew over the
Cuckoo's Nest* (both 1975) proved the George Hanson role was not a
fluke. In the 80s and 90s, his acting was equally varied in *The Shining*
(1980), *Reds* (1981), *Terms of Endearment* (1983), *Prizzi's Honor* (1985),
Batman (1989), *Wolf* (1994) and *The Crossing Guard* (1995). Nicholson
remains a mainstream superstar who retains subversive credentials.

As each year passes, it is clear that the success and promise of *Easy
Rider* and the BBS films were ultimately significant for the freedom and
access they allowed for a group of directors dubbed the 'Movie Brats'.
Coppola, Lucas, Spielberg, DePalma, Scorsese and Paul Schrader were
true Hollywood outsiders. They had no studio connections, but lots of
drive and talent. Educated in college and university film programs in
New York and California, they created the blockbusters which became
the new model for studio production. Their films – *Jaws* (1975), *Close
Encounters of the Third Kind* (1977), *The Godfather Parts I and II* (1971,
1974), *Taxi Driver* (1976), *Carrie* (1976), *Star Wars* (1977) and
Apocalypse Now (1979) – represent an astonishing fusion of popular

genres and personal expressiveness. The success of *Easy Rider* can also be said to have contributed to the success of the radical and often experimental 70s films of older directors such as Robert Altman, Milos Forman and Alan Pakula.

The 70s were a liberating and expansive period for Hollywood. The decision makers at the studios became younger and took bigger risks. American film-makers were encouraged to explore an unparalleled range of genres and themes. The diversity, maturity and sophistication of both studio and independent releases from the United States compared favourably with acclaimed films from Germany, France, Italy and Australia in the same decade.

Yet perversely the New Hollywood evolved, in the 80s, into more of a conservative monolith than the old Hollywood had been. The blockbuster encouraged the growth of lavish spectacles, driven by expensive stars and special effects. The small, personal film bred by *Easy Rider* and BBS became an anachronism. Even the narrative certainty of *Casablanca* (1942) and *Treasure of the Sierra Madre* (1948) began to look avant-garde, as studios looked for films that could be explained by a simple sentence or one word. Hollywood is now more concerned with billion-dollar multimedia mergers, merchandising spin-offs, and ancillary rights on video and cable.

Easy Rider and the vitality of subsequent American film-making in the 70s almost, but not quite, achieved Godard's dream of one film for everybody. In this synthesis of the mass media, art and politics, a cinema flourished that both encapsulated and diverted the energy of the 60s counter-culture. These films succeeded in capturing the zeitgeist, but they also seemed to succumb, perhaps too easily, to the despair and cynicism spawned by Watergate and the disaster in Vietnam. Neither *Easy Rider* nor other key 70s films encouraged much in the way of activism or commitment to a cause or purpose.

In an eloquent retrospective essay in the July 1981 *Esquire*, American journalist and political commentator Jeff Greenfield found the political failure of *Easy Rider* and, by association, the New Hollywood, ironic: 'It may not have been *Easy Rider*'s intention to stand as the statement of a generation, or as anything so pretentious. But the fact that so many could accept the film as just that may explain why the 70s culminated in the landslide triumph of a man and an idea that so fundamentally reject the vision of this film.'[27]

That man was Ronald Reagan and that vision was a brand of Malthusian conservatism that continues to have repercussions not just in the United States, but in Canada, much of Europe, Latin America, and the Pacific Rim Countries of Southeast Asia. *Easy Rider* shifted the consciousness of the baby-boom generation, but George Hanson didn't win in the voting booth or box office. In the summer of 1994, baby boomers flocked to *Forrest Gump*, a recantation and revision of 60s radicalism and idealism as simply an adolescent phase. Its manipulative self-help rhetoric ('Life is just a box of chocolates') somehow managed to convince many viewers that the blind naivety of a country simpleton was the zenith of political awareness. The sound of Voltaire turning in his grave was audible in less deluded quarters.

In spite of its eventual political limitations, it is hard not to think of *Easy Rider* as *the* road movie. Many fine, noble and informed arguments can be constructed to demonstrate that it was not the first film to explore the menace and romance of the American highway, but since the summer of 1969, *Easy Rider* has the iconic edge. It identified the road movie as a flexible genre, capable of accommodating a wide range of complex themes. On one hand, it is characterised by a romantic depiction of the speed and machinery of cars and motorbikes, the seemingly limitless opportunities of modern travel, and the celebration of individuals improvising and exploring their identity. But on the other hand, the road movie also reveals the elusiveness of liberty in an over-industrialised world, the homogenisation of experience in a global economy, and the alienation and oppression suffered by many who live in this brave new world. *Easy*

Rider contained these characteristics and themes by the truckload.

It would be impossible to deal with all of the post-*Easy Rider* road movies within this book, but there are several titles, both famous and obscure, worth mentioning to demonstrate how the genre flourished after the killing of Billy and Wyatt.

The BBS films were almost all road movies of a kind (even Jaglom's *A Safe Place* (1971) is arguably a road movie of the mind). Monte Hellman's *Two-Lane Blacktop* (1971) from an original screenplay by Rudy Wurlitzer, depicted a meaningless cross-country race between Warren Oates and two drag racers played by James Taylor and Dennis Wilson. Terrence Malick's *Badlands* (1974) followed two amoral killers on a killing spree in Dakota during the 50s. Hal Ashby explored the life of the peripatetic folksinger Woody Guthrie in *Bound for Glory* (1978).

In Canada, Don Shebib made *Going Down the Road* (1970) to dramatise the social and economic inequalities of two young men from Newfoundland trying to find work in Toronto. James Frawley's rarely screened *The Christian Licorice Store* (1971) was almost a docudrama about the lives of the BBS crowd. Steven Spielberg used the road movie to make two of his darkest entertainments, *Duel* (1972) and *Sugarland*

Forrest Gump, a dispiriting recantation of 60s radicalism and idealism.

Express (1974). Richard Sarafian's *Vanishing Point* (1971) and John Hough's *Dirty Mary, Crazy Larry* (1974), featuring Peter Fonda, and Michael Cimino's *Thunderbolt and Lightfoot* (1974) were enthusiastic variations on Roger Corman's exploitation flick aesthetic. Sydney Pollack placed racing car driver, Al Pacino, against the glittering spas of Europe in *Bobby Deerfield* (1976). Altman's *Thieves Like Us* (1973) revisited the source material of Nicholas Ray's *They Live by Night* (1948) and heightened the Depression era setting. Scorsese's *Alice Doesn't Live Here Anymore* (1974) was not only his only road movie, but a rare exploration of feminist concerns within the genre. Sam Peckinpah's *The Getaway* (1972), based on the Jim Thompson novel, pushed the genre's anti-authoritarian stance to the limit with the casting of Ali McGraw and Steve McQueen as sexy anti-heroes. Howard Zieff's *Slither* (1973) from a script by W. D. Richter was an off-beat comedy that played with popular fears of rural America's wide spaces and small towns. Comedy was also explored in Paul Mazursky's unusually gentle *Harry and Tonto* (1974) and Bogdanovich's nostalgic *Paper Moon* (1973).

In Germany, Wim Wenders was so obsessed with the genre that he named his production company Road Movies. As a reviewer for *Filmkritik*, he wrote a collage-like rave review of *Easy Rider* and would later cast Hopper in *The American Friend*. He gained international attention with both this thriller and his trilogy of road movies, *Alice in the Cities* (1974), *Wrong Movement* (1975) and *Kings of the Road* (1976), which explored West Germany's complex post-war relationship with America. In turn, he co-produced *Radio On* (1979), the debut of Chris Petit, a critic for London's *Time Out.* The fact that Petit was able to make a road movie rooted in English concerns of class and repression speaks volumes about the genre's malleability.

The road movie has had many subtle variations in Europe from Barbet Schroeder's explorations of the international hippie culture, *More* (1970) and *The Valley* (1972), to Agnes Varda's study of a disturbed young woman, *Vagabond* (1985), Alain Corneau's *Nocturne indien* (1989) and Theo Angelopoulos' revelatory *Landscape in the Mist* (1988). The concept of 'lighting out for the territory' has a completely different complex of associations in a Europe dealing with centuries of tradition, historical conflicts, and the cumulative effects of commerce and industrialisation. The European films emphasise the futility of escape on the road. Spiritual faith and the imagination are seen as the only true starting points for a journey.

As mainstream Hollywood turned away from personal film-making in the 80s and 90s, mavericks working on the fringe and independent directors used the road movie to explore unpopular themes and issues. Rudy Wurlitzer and Robert Frank collaborated on *Candy Mountain* (1986), a 'Northern' which moves from New York to the remote fishing towns of Nova Scotia. Ross McElwee wore a camera throughout his search for love in the autobiographical documentary *Sherman's March* (1985). Jonathan Demme's *Something Wild* (1986) was an unsettling combination of travelogue, romance, comedy and psychological thriller. David Lynch and novelist Barry Gifford reversed *Easy Rider*'s trip in *Wild at Heart* (1990) by starting from Cape Fear in the South and ending up in Los Angeles. Their heroes encounter violence at almost every stop. Ultra-violence is *the* subject of Tony's Scott's *True Romance* (1993), Oliver Stone's *Natural Born Killers* (1994), scripted by pop culture junkie/auteur Quentin Tarantino, and Gregg Araki's *The Living End* (1993), shot on 16mm. Canadian director Bruce McDonald brought a similar trash aesthetic to *Roadkill* (1990) and *Highway 61* (1992). Bill MacGillivray's *Stations* (1983) is, by contrast, an unusually subdued road movie as character study. Two of the finest road films in recent years, Gus Van Sant's *My Own Private Idaho* (1991) and Carl Franklin's *One False Move* (1992) combine a rich commentary on sexuality and race with visual designs that borrow freely from European, avant-garde and Hollywood styles.

Martin Brest, Barry Levinson or Ridley Scott aren't known as maverick directors, but their respective road movies, *Midnight Run* (1988), *Rain Man* (1988), and *Thelma and Louise* (1992) have been their most challenging works for a mass audience. Callie Khouri's screenplay

(Overleaf) *Easy Rider* inspired road movies up to *Thelma and Louise* and beyond.

for *Thelma and Louise* paid direct homage to *Easy Rider* with its famous ending of Susan Sarandon and Geena Davis driving their car off a cliff to escape the police. For a slick star-driven film, the ending was refreshingly unresolved. The film's popularity confirmed that there is still a vital danger in the genre.

———————

Given such a rich legacy, can one get away with calling *Easy Rider* a classic, a great work of art? *Easy Rider* does not lend itself easily to snap conclusions. In his *LA Free Press* review of July 25 1969, future writer and director, Paul Schrader argued: 'Easy Rider is a very important movie – and it is also a very bad one, and I don't think its importance should be used to underestimate the gross mismanagement of its subject matter.' He found the film 'slick and superficial, a sop to liberal guilt and underground paranoia'. At the time his review caused so much outrage among his readers and peers that he was fired.[28] Now that the film has lost much of its counter-culture associations and become something else, one wonders if he would write a different review.

Easy Rider almost single-handedly created the road movie as a vital post-60s genre, but it did lose the greater revolution of changing mainstream studio production and deeply affecting the consciousness of the majority of its viewers. By anticipating this outcome, the film's fatalism anticipates and embodies many of the criticisms levelled at it. If great art is supposed to be rich enough to contain a multitude of contradictions, as well as a richness of theme and subtext, then *Easy Rider* is a great film. While its director lacks the authoritative assurance that marks the work of a Jean Renoir, John Ford or Stanley Kubrick, this reservation affirms that *Easy Rider* is not just the vision of one man. It was the creation of a highly talented collective, and the dynamic that informed their debate was extended to the audience.

Easy Rider uncannily documents an era that was in the process of ending before it ever truly began. At the 1968 Chicago Democratic

Convention, demonstrators, captured by TV news cameras, chanted 'The Whole World Is Watching'. In 1992, at the Republican Convention, Pat Buchanan made his notorious 'there is a war going on in the streets of America' speech. *Easy Rider* is the kind of film that makes you speculate how many in the audience were at both conventions.

Watching *Easy Rider* from the perspective of my mid-30s, I cannot detach myself from my vague childhood memories of the film's initial release. I grew up with the film second hand via late-night TV and repertory screenings. A powerful elegiac quality, as well as a certain masochism, inform each viewing. I am not nostalgic for the 60s. The past always seems like a golden era when one is safely past its immediate chaos. However, I am affected by the *Easy Rider*'s demonstration of how impossible and cruel the dreams of cinema can be. I always hope Billy,

Easy Rider: a road well travelled or a road not taken?

Wyatt, George, the commune dwellers, Mary and Karen, and the rest are going to make it. Similarily, I hope another film like *Easy Rider* comes along even if the window of cinema's possibility seems barely open as its centenary passes. The road may no longer be so well travelled, but it is still open, wide and free for those who wish to take it.

Notes

1 Estimate given by Susan Sackett, *The Hollywood Reporter Book of Box Office Hits* (New York: Billboard Books, 1990), p. 206.

2 Peter Fonda interviewed by Nick Jones, *Born To Be Wild*, BBC2 documentary, broadcast 16 Dec. 1995. Quotations are taken from rough footage supplied to the author.

3 Interview with Terry Southern by the author, October 1993.

4 References to the shooting script of *Easy Rider* are based on two very similar drafts from January–February 1968. The first was shown to the author by Terry Southern, and the other is located in the BFI archives.

5 Peter Fonda and Dennis Hopper, *Born To Be Wild* documentary.

6 Interview with Southern, see n. 3.

7 Fonda, *Born To Be Wild* documentary.

8 Actress Karen Black, *Born To Be Wild* documentary.

9 *Easy Rider* shooting script in Southern archives.

10 Hopper, *Born To Be Wild* documentary.

11 Letter to Terry Southern, 6 March 1968, Southern archives.

12 'Interview with Laszlo Kovacs', in Dennis Schaefer and Larry Salvato (eds), *Masters of Light: Conversations with Contemporary Cinematographers* (Berkeley: University of California Press, 1984), p. 181.

13 Letter from Southern to Peter Fonda, 24 April 1968, Southern archives.

14 Henry Jaglom, *Born To Be Wild* documentary.

15 Interview with Southern, see n. 3.

16 Fonda, *Born To Be Wild* documentary, and David Fricke, 'Interview with Roger McGuinn', *Rolling Stone*, 23 August 1990, p. 146.

17 'Keeping the Beat: Interview with Donn Cambern', in Gabriella Oldham (ed.), *First Cut: Conversations with Film Editors* (Berkeley: University of California Press, 1992), p. 206.

18 Interview with Southern, see n. 3. Southern also waived his profit participation in the film during the writing stage.

19 Susan Sackett, *Hollywood Reporter Book of Box Office Hits*, pp. 202–7.

20 Fonda mentions Hesse's book in the *Born To Be Wild* documentary.

21 Unless otherwise indicated, all dialogue quoted in this section is taken from the film.

22 Terry Southern, 'Red Dirt Marijuana', *Red Dirt Marijuana and Other Tastes* (New York: New American Library, 1967; reissued by Citadel Underground, 1990), p. 13.

23 Terry Southern, 'Razor Fight', *Red Dirt Marijuana and Other Tastes*.

24 *Easy Rider* shooting
script, BFI archives.

25 Tom Burke, 'Dennis
Hopper Saves the Movies',
Esquire, September 1970,
p. 170.

26 Interview with Michael
O'Donoghue by the author,
March 1993.

27 Jeff Greenfield,
'Retrospective: Easy
Rider', *Esquire*, July 1981,
pp. 90–1.

28 Paul Schrader, 'Easy
Rider', in Kevin Jackson
(ed.), *Schrader on
Schrader* (London: Faber
and Faber, 1990),
pp. 34–7.

Credits

EASY RIDER

USA
1969

Director
Dennis Hopper

Production companies
Raybert Productions
A Pando Company in
association with Raybert
Productions presentation
A Columbia Pictures
Release

World premiere
Cannes Film Festival,
13 May 1969

US premiere
10 July 1969

Executive producer
Bert Schneider

Producer
Peter Fonda

Associate producer
William L. Hayward

Production manager
Paul Lewis

Location manager
Tony Vorno

Post production
Marilyn Schlossberg

Script supervisor
Joyce King

Assistant director
Len Marshal

Screenplay
Peter Fonda, Dennis
Hopper and Terry Southern

Consultant
Henry Jaglom

Photography
Laszlo Kovacs

Assistant Camera
Peter Heiser, Jr.

Key grip
Thomas Ramsey

Gaffer
Richmond Aguilar

Electrician
Foster Denker

Best boy
Mel Maxwell

Stills
Peter Sorel

Editor
Donn Cambern

Assistant editor
Stanley Siegel

Art director
Jerry Kay

Make-up
Virgil Frye

Special effects
Steve Karkus

Titles
Cinefx

Stunt gaffer
Tex Hall

Property Master
Robert O'Neil

Transportation
Lee Pierpont

Generator
Guy Badger

Music editing
Synchrofilm Inc.

Songs:
Steppenwolf, 'Pusher',
composed by Hoyt Axton
Steppenwolf, 'Born To Be
Wild', composed by Mars
Bonfire
The Byrds, 'Wasn't Born To
Follow', composed by
Gerry Coffin and Carole
King
The Band, 'The Weight',
composed by J. Robbie
Robertson
The Holy Modal Rounders,
'If You Want To Be A Bird',
composed by Antonia
Duren
Fraternity of Men, 'Don't
Bogart Me', composed by
Elliot Ingber and
Larry Wagner
The Jimi Hendrix
Experience, 'If Six Was
Nine', composed by
Jimi Hendrix
Little Eva, 'Let's Turkey
Trot', composed by Gerry
Coffin and Jack Keller
The Electric Prunes, 'Kyrie
Eleison', composed by
David Axelrod
The Electric Flag, 'Flash,
Bam, Pow', composed by
Mike Bloomfield
Roger McGuinn, 'It's
Alright Ma (I'm Only
Bleeding)', composed by
Bob Dylan
Roger McGuinn, 'The
Ballad of Easy Rider',
composed by
Roger McGuinn

Sound
Ryder Sound Service Inc.

Sound mixer
Le Roy Robbins

Sound boom
James Contrares

Sound effects
Edit-Rite Inc.

Re-recording
Producers' Sound Service
Inc.

95 minutes
8,535 feet

Peter Fonda
Wyatt

Dennis Hopper
Billy

Antonio Mendoza
Jesus

Phil Spector
Connection

Mac Mashourian
Bodyguard

Warren Finnerty
Rancher

Tita Colorado
Rancher's wife

Luke Askew
Stranger on highway

Commune:

Luana Anders
Lisa

Sabrina Scharf
Sarah

Sandy Wyeth
Joanne

Robert Walker
Jack

Robert Ball
Carmen Phillips
Ellie Walker
Michael Pataki
Mimes

Jail:

Jack Nicholson
George Hanson

George Fowler, Jr.
Guard

Keith Green
Sheriff

Cafe:

Hayward Roubillard
Cat man

Arnold Hess, Jr.
Deputy

Buddy Causey, Jr.
Duffy LaFont
Blase M. Dawson
Paul Guedry, Jr.
Customers

Suzie Ramagos
Elida Ann Hebert
Rose LeBlanc
Mary Kay Hebert
Cynthia Grezaffi
Colette Purpera
Girls

Madame Tinkertoy's House
of Blue Lights:

Toni Basil
Mary

Karen Black
Karen

Lee Marmer
Madame

Cathe Cozzi
Dancing girl

Thea Salerno
Anne McClain
Beatriz Monteil
Marcia Bowman
Hookers

Pick-up truck:

David C. Billodeau
1st Man

Johnny David
2nd man

Bibliography

Easy Rider production information was taken from a number of sources, most notably interviews supplied to the author by Nick Jones from his BBC2 documentary *Born To Be Wild* (1995). Interviews with Terry Southern and Michael O'Donoghue were conducted by the author in March and October, 1993. Production correspondence and script drafts pertaining to *Easy Rider* were supplied by Southern from his archives. Also valuable were the liner notes to the Columbia laser disc of *Easy Rider*, released in October 1995.

Tom Burke, 'Dennis Hopper Saves the Movies', *Esquire*, September 1970, pp. 139–72.

Seth Cagin, and Paul Dray, *Born To Be Wild* (formerly titled *Hollywood Films of the Seventies*) (New York: Harper and Row, 1984; reissued and revised, 1995).

L. M. Kit Carson. 'Easy Rider: A Very American Film: An Interview with Dennis Hopper', *Evergreen Review* vol. 13 no. 72., November 1969, pp. 26–7, 70–2.

Peter Collier, *The Fondas* (New York: Putnam, 1991).

Bernard Dick (ed.), *Columbia: Portrait of a Studio* (Lexington, Kentucky: University of Kentucky Press, 1992).

Peter Fonda, Dennis Hopper and Terry Southern, *Easy Rider* shooting script 1968, located in BFI archives.

Peter Fonda, Dennis Hopper, and Terry Southern, *Easy Rider: The Complete Screenplay*, ed. Nancy Hardin and Marilyn Schlossberg (New York: Signet, 1969). Book actually contains the cutting continuity not a version of the shooting script.

David Fricke, 'Interview with Roger McGuinn', *Rolling Stone*, 23 August 1990, pp. 107–10, 146.

Todd Gitlin, *The Sixties: Days of Hope, Days of Rage* (New York: Bantam, 1987; revised edition, 1993).

Mike Golden, 'Now Dig This: Interview with Terry Southern', *Reflex Magazine*, September, 1992.

Michael Goodwin, 'Camera: Laszlo Kovacs', *Take One*, October 1971, pp. 12–16.

Lawrence Linderman, 'Playboy Interview with Peter Fonda', *Playboy*, September 1970, pp. 85–106, 278–9.

Patrick McGilligan. *Jack's Life: A Biography of Jack Nicholson* (New York: W. W. Norton, 1994).

Linda Miles and Michael Pye, *The Movie Brats* (New York: Holt, Rinehart and Winston, 1979).

James Monaco, *American Film Now* (New York: New American Library/Plume, 1979; revised edition, 1984).

Gabriella Oldham (ed.),
'Keeping the Beat:
Interview with Donn
Cambern', *First Cut:
Conversations with Film
Editors* (Berkeley and Los
Angeles: University of
California Press, 1992).

Tony Rief and Iain Ewing.
'Interview with Peter
Fonda', *Take One* vol. 2
no. 3, 1969, pp. 6–10.

Elena Rodriguez, *Dennis
Hopper: A Madness to His
Method* (New York: St
Martin's Press, 1988).

Susan Sackett, *The
Hollywood Reporter Book
of Box Office Hits*
(New York: Billboard
Books, 1990).

Denis Schaefer and Larry
Salvato (eds), 'Interview
with Laszlo Kovacs',
*Masters of Light:
Conversations with
Contemporary
Cinematographers*
(Berkeley: University of
California Press, 1984).

Terry Southern, Letter to
the Editor (re: *Easy Rider*
improvisations), *The New
York Times*, 7 June 1970.

Terry Southern, *Red Dirt
Marijuana and Other Tastes*
(New York: New American
Library, 1967). Reissued by
Citadel Underground in
1990 with an introduction
by George Plimpton.

Wim Wenders, *Emotion
Pictures: Reflections on the
Cinema* (London: Faber
and Faber, 1986).

Mark Williams, *Road
Movies* (New York: Proteus,
1982).